HOW TO HEAL

A Practical Guide To Nine Natural Therapies
You Can Use To Release Your Trauma

Jessi Beyer

Praise for How To Heal

ભ્રઃ

"Vindicating…Beyer's sensitive prose will ease concerns of other trauma survivors. Those seeking additional help with their own trauma recovery will want to take a look."

– PUBLISHER'S WEEKLY

"I read through your book and learned SO MUCH! You touched on therapies that I have been interested in and loved your approach to discussing them. I loved the way that you handled each and the multiple approaches to each and above all the respect for the person who was healing – beautifully done! Throughout you showed so much respect for people going through this process, both those healing from the trauma and those supporting them! Your book is beautiful and rich and full of helpful insight. THANK YOU! Your book has already made a difference in how I work with people with trauma and will continue to do so! THANK YOU!"

– HEATHER JEFFREY, MA, LADC, CTC

"Right from the beginning, *How To Heal* introduces us to the authors trauma story in an authentic and vulnerable narrative. Her personal journey into the healing process informs the book throughout as she takes us to discover an array of exciting therapeutic interventions emerging over recent decades all of which share the backing of a growing body of empirical evidence and inquiry. She weaves a non-pharmacological web of integrative therapies deftly colored in by her matter-of-fact and practical testimony. The undersong of the book is clear: among the pain there is power; among the ordinary there is hope. The honesty of her experience is inspirational to all of us who have experienced (or know of someone who has experienced) trauma. I say 'read it'. You'll uncover a treasure chest filled with gems."

– JEAN LARSON, PHD, HTR, CTRS

"Jessi Beyer speaks directly to the trauma survivor in this terrific and encouraging review of avenues for healing that go beyond conventional talk therapy."

– ALEX JORDAN, PH.D., MCLEAN HOSPITAL AND HARVARD MEDICAL SCHOOL

"This was a thoroughly enjoyable read, and one of incredible clinical value. In the counseling world, there are a variety of theories, techniques, and interventions that are used to treat trauma. Among other things, Jessi Beyer has provided a very human and relatable understanding of how we experience trauma, while also providing an expert view of some of the more modern treatments for trauma. More importantly, many of these interventions focus on our common humanity and how we can heal in a very natural way. The final chapter, What therapy might work for me, offers some essential guidance that could help many of our clients make more personalized treatment decisions. I recommend picking this one up."

– PATRICK POWELL ED. D, NCC., LMHC. (FL), QS (FL). LPC (TN), CCSOTS

"How To Heal beautifully adds to the much-needed dialogue about mental health. Beyer provides practical approaches to an often untouched subject in a relatable manner. This book is a valuable resource for both trauma survivors and supporters of survivors. Thank you, Jessi, for sharing your story and using your experiences to help others."

– SAVANNAH WIX, MISS ARIZONA USA 2019

"Just the first read through of your experience alone has given me chills and also helps me to entrust you as someone who can offer healing to those who deal with these struggles, both as a trauma survivor and a professional. I'm so proud to endorse this book. For those wishing to gain deeper understanding of how to handle one's own struggles through therapy and how to be of help to another in a healthy way, this book is for you!"

– TIANNA TUAMOHELOA, MISS NEVADA USA 2019

"Jessi Beyer shares such a stunningly courageous and intimate view of what trauma looks and feels like for women. This book is so needed to help women young and old understand how trauma therapy works and how much more effective it is for healing us than traditional talk therapy. It is time for the rest of the world to understand what many of us have been training and doing for many decades –healing trauma through the body safely. This book is a wonderful contribution to getting that important healing news to more women now!"

– DONNA ROE DANIELL, LCSW, RYT, AUTHOR OF
HANDBOOK TO MIDLIFE CHALLENGES FOR WOMEN

"Beyer takes the reader by the hand and personally shows them how to manage their painful story. In an extremely reader-friendly fashion, Jessi Beyer introduces you to her personal experience of trauma. Beyer shares her breakthroughs and lessons learned on her own journey, writing from one trauma survivor to another. *How To Heal* is an engaging, hands-on guide to understanding trauma-and stressor-related disorders. This practical and useful book is also valuable for family and friends of those who are traumatized. As a thanatologist, I have seen how suicide and other traumatic losses, impact the lives of clients. For that reason, I also highly recommend this book for clinicians who care about Trauma-Informed Care."

– BARBARA RUBEL, MA, BCETS, D.A.A.E.T.S.

"Jessi Beyer has crafted the perfect resource for those looking for effective ways to release their trauma. It provides a wealth of practical information about therapies that target trauma and go beyond the traditional psychotherapy approach."

– DEBRA BURDICK, LCSW, AUTHOR OF
MINDFULNESS SKILLS WORKBOOK

"Insightful, refreshingly honest and captivating. A must-read for anyone looking to expand their knowledge on trauma-related issues."

– MICHAEL CASEY, MENTAL HEALTH ADVOCATE
AND AUTHOR OF *BREAKING FREE*

"*How to Heal* by Jessi Beyer is a book we ALL need no matter where you are in your healing journey. We all have trauma and a majority of us never get to the root of how our mind works and how it effects our daily lives, choices, and relationships. By sharing her experiences of her personal trauma, *How To Heal* feels like the comfort of a best friend guiding you with open arms. Let's take time to heal so we can grow, together. Beyer will give you the tools to live with the peace of mind you've always longed for."

– BROOKE JOHNSON, MISS ALASKA USA 2018, NAMI
AMBASSADOR AND WESTSIDE LOS ANGELES
PRESENTER

"As someone who works closely within the mental health field, I know how hard discussing the topic can be. I commend you for your honesty in sharing your experience. *How To Heal* has already expanded my mind a great deal and has helped my understanding even further from a survivor's prospective, especially on my own journey as a survivor and advocate of domestic violence."

– JONÉT NICHELLE, MISS RHODE ISLAND USA 2020

This book is being given to

_____

because you've fought battles no one can see, you hold an inner strength greater than many can ever imagine, and you're ready to finally win the war.

DOWNLOAD THE AUDIOBOOK FOR FREE!

READ THIS FIRST

Just to say thanks for purchasing *How To Heal*, I would like to give you the audiobook version 100% FREE!

TO DOWNLOAD GO TO:

https://www.jessibeyerinternational.com/audiobook

Table of Contents

ෆ෩

INTRODUCTION TO TRAUMA

TRAUMA HEALING METHODS

AFTEREFFECTS AND HELPING OTHERS

Chapter 1:
My Experience with
Trauma
᎒᎒

I can remember the exact place I was standing when I noticed the scars on my friend's inner forearm: the start of the 200m race on my high school's track, facing backwards, lined up and getting ready to run some ladders for agility drills. I also remember exactly what I said to him when I saw them: "Do you have a cat?" He said no. He actually had a cat, but I realize now that his "no" was answering the question that I wanted to ask but didn't. That deeper "no" was also a lie.

It took a few weeks for him to open up to me about his depression, self-harm, and suicidal tendencies. I was about ready to finish up my sophomore year of high school, and from that point onward, I felt the weight of the world on my shoulders. In actuality, it was the weight of his world that I placed on my shoulders. Over the next year and a half, I became his

1

confidante. Every time he struggled, he called me. Every time he cut himself, he called me. Every time he got stuck in his head, he called me. I believed I was responsible for protecting his privacy and honoring his trust in me, which meant I was lying to my mom, lying to his mom, and lying to the school's counselor. At the time, I was so thankful. I felt important, and I felt like I was making an impact. I felt like I was responsible for his happiness and mental health, and I felt like a success because I believed I was maintaining it. I believed I was the reason he was staying alive.

It turned out that I wasn't bringing him up – he was dragging me down. I remember the first time I cut myself. It was August 12, the day before my junior season of soccer started. I remember the second time I drew blood when I cut. I called him because I freaked out, and I remember he told me that it would become easier to see the blood each time you drew it. I remember being calmed down by him saying that. I also remember all of the times I gave him my body to kiss, to feel, and to be on top of because I believed that if I kept him happy and gave him what he wanted, he would stay alive. I remember being proud of the fact that I would do literally whatever it took for him to stay alive.

I made him promise me that he would give me a hug before he took his own life. It was my way of having some control over the situation so I could stop it, but I told him it was so that I could hold him while he left this earth. I remember the exact moment that he texted me and told me to come give him a hug and say goodbye. I was eating some chicken in my kitchen. I was the only one home. I had just gotten home from school. I vividly remember dropping the chicken on the counter and falling to the floor when I received that text, but the drive to his house is a complete blur. I know I was speeding. I know I majorly cut someone off getting off the highway. I know that I called my aunt, who is a psychologist, along the way to ask for her help. She told me to call the police and to prepare myself to walk into his house and find him dead. I remember listening to her.

The 911 dispatcher told me to wait for the police to arrive before going into the house because she was worried he would hurt me. I knew she was wrong. He would never hurt me. The cops, when they showed up, were less than helpful. They were only concerned with whether he and I were sexually intimate, and they paid no heed to the fact that I was frantic he was about to kill himself. He kept texting me, asking where I was, asking if I was coming. I kept having to make up lies, telling him that I was on my way, that I got stuck at a red light, and that I made a wrong turn, knowing that I was sitting a block away from his house, completely helpless to the fact that I knew he had a knife and a bottle of Aspirin in his hands.

While the cops were asking me about our sexual relationship, my mom got home. I might have texted her while I was driving and told her what was going on, but I honestly don't remember. All I remember is her screaming at me over the phone, cussing at me, and telling me that she needed to be there. I wanted to do this alone, and I didn't feel that I was capable of managing her emotions while dealing with the situation in front of me, so she was instructed to wait for me in a local shopping mall.

When the police finally gave me the okay to approach the house, I walked too fast and too far ahead of them, and they whistled at me to slow down and wait for them. Though I can't claim to read the minds of the police officers, all their treatment of me did was made me feel like I was overreacting and that my friend's situation wasn't worth serious concern. I remember ringing his doorbell and having him open the door, but I was too ashamed to meet his eyes. I remember whispering "I'm sorry" and stepping out of the way so the cops could do their job. That night ended with me texting his mom, "You need to come home. He just tried to kill himself.", his dad cancelling a business trip, and him being led out of the house in handcuffs.

I remember the first time I heard from him after that night. A text: "I trusted you."

That night broke me. I suppose that my precarious mental state didn't help matters, either, but it has taken me years to believe that I did the right thing that night. I knew how betrayed and angry I would have felt if he did that to me, so I knew I hurt him in the deadliest way that I could have. I took away his control. I know, logically, that I did the right thing. His mom believes that I saved his life, and she's thankful for me. I'm learning to be thankful for me, too.

I went to one day of therapy. I was seventeen. I was so uncomfortable, sitting in this chair and having a stranger pick me apart to the depths of my soul. I didn't trust her. I didn't want to tell her my story. I wanted to get as far away from that tiny room as I possibly could, but I also wanted to get better. I just knew that that environment would not be helpful for me.

I was also absolutely terrified that the therapist would tell my mom that I cut myself, so I lied and downplayed my situation. The therapist diagnosed me with Adjustment Disorder and said that we didn't have to tell my mom anything I said. I felt both relieved and rejected by that statement. I literally ran out of that therapy session and never went back.

I could write a whole book about my relationship with this individual, how it impacted me then, and how it's still impacting me now, but that's not the point of this book. Maybe that will be the next one. I'm writing this book because I was in your position. I have an undergraduate degree in psychology and have interviewed many professionals on the topic of trauma, but I am not writing this book as a professional telling you what to do with your life and your healing journey. I am writing this book as one trauma survivor speaking to another and because I wish that I had known what I'm going to share with you here. I wish I knew that there were other options for therapy than sitting on a couch and having someone stare into the depths of your soul. I wish I knew how to handle my friends and family members as I was healing (and I wish they knew how to help me, too). I wish I knew all of the wonderful people that I've talked to while writing this book; I wish I knew that there were people like them to help me when I needed it most.

I'm writing this book because someone needs to tell you those things. Someone needs to tell you that you're not broken and that your trauma is worthy of healing from. Someone to tell you that there are options for healing from the pain, the anger, the guilt, and the sorrow that do not involve talk therapy. Someone to tell you what happens during therapy so it's not so scary walking into it. Someone to tell you that you are loved, and accepted, and *right*, no matter how wrong you feel. My hope is that, through my writing and your reading of this book, you can take the first steps toward healing in a way that honors you and is comfortable for you. There is so much understanding to be gained from these pages, about trauma and about ways that you can heal, and I hope that you're able to glean enough of it that you can start your own healing journey. Understand what trauma is and what it does. Learn about the different options of healing from it. Pick one that feels the best to you and finally, *finally*, learn to heal. There's so much life waiting for you on the other side.

Chapter 2:
What Is Trauma?

⳩⳨

When you hear the word trauma, what do you think of? A veteran struggling with PTSD? A rape victim terrified of intimate contact? A near-death experience, like a horrible car accident? Whatever you think of, I want you to wipe it from your mind. The real question to ask is not what trauma is, but what trauma isn't. Trauma is such an individual experience that it's nearly impossible to classify what is and what isn't trauma. The reason for this is that every single individual responds to an incident in a different way, and trauma lies more in how the individual reacts to a situation than in what the situation was. In other words, while Jane may not consider getting assaulted on her way home from class that big of a deal, Mary may consider it extremely traumatic. For Mary, that assault was a trauma, but not for Jane. It often boils down to whether the individual felt like they were able find a way to feel like they were in control, like they were not alone, and like they were safe. If they were, they are often not traumatized by the event; if they weren't, then that usually becomes a trauma to that person.

It's critical to remember this, because categorizing trauma or trying to compare its severity between individuals or circumstances can be detrimental to both parties. When I spoke with Heather Jeffrey, Sally Mixon, and Lynn Moore at Acres for Life, an equine-assisted therapy facility in Forest Lake, Minnesota, I asked them to speak on the fact that many individuals try diminishing the trauma response in themselves or other people. You know what I mean – it's the "there are starving children in Africa so how dare you complain about your own life" criticism, and I'd bet that you either have been told that or have said that to yourself before. When I explained this concept to them and asked their professional opinion on it, I wish I could have captured their responding facial expressions. Their expressions were enough of a response, but I'll do my best to sum it up in words: confused, disgusted, and aghast are the best words I can find. They then went on to say that it's impossible and unethical to compare severities of trauma due to the individuality of the trauma response and the detriment that such a comparison can cause on the healing process. For example, telling Mary that the assault wasn't that big of a deal and that she's being dramatic is completely disrespectful to her and her experience, and can be a huge hindrance in her healing, as she'll begin to believe that there's something wrong with her for feeling the way she does. On the other hand, telling Jane that an assault is a traumatic experience can hinder her because then she, too, begins to believe something's wrong with her because she didn't react emotionally to the assault.

The same goes for you when you're talking or thinking about your trauma. Whether other people think what happened to you was traumatic or not, you have every right to own your emotions and own your trauma. It is your story, and only you can understand the depth and breadth by which you're affected. Sally, when she was discussing this, said that it's an "intimate, beautiful piece of being human" (as you'll start to see here, one of the goals of this book is to reshape how you view your trauma and help you recognize the positives in your experience – so don't slam the cover and think I'm disrespecting your pain and trauma quite yet!). It is a part of your journey, and you – and your journey – are beautiful and worthy of complete acceptance. There's no need to or benefit in comparing levels of severity of the trauma or trying to decide if you're overreacting. I've been there, and all it does it suck you down in this spiral of shame and confusion. You can't begin to heal when you're stuck there.

But, as I've said before, if you experienced what most people consider a traumatic incident – rape, assault, kidnapping, war, et cetera – and you're not feeling the need to heal because it didn't affect you, that's also just fine. You do not need to fit in some pre-determined trauma box. Basically, what I'm trying to say is that your reaction to whatever traumatic event happened to you is completely okay, completely valid, and completely deserving of healing. Never forget that.

I had a few friends in high school that I thought could be support systems for me, and I ruined that by falling prey to comparing traumas. One of my friends had a severe eating disorder and the other had attempted suicide a number of times, but I didn't know this when I first began talking to them about my story. As soon as I found it out, I decided that I was unworthy of their help because they'd been through so much worse. I felt like I was complaining about nothing when they had real scars, real battle stories to tell. Needless to say, that ruined my supportive relationship with them and put them in a box that only they were qualified to put themselves in. I learned my lesson from that, and I'm hoping that by my brief story, you won't have to alienate potential support systems by comparing traumas like I did.

That all being said, I believe it's important to define trauma to an extent, because there are characteristics of trauma and its healing process that differ from other mental health struggles. The way one heals from trauma is different than the way one heals from schizophrenia, for example. Heather put it beautifully when she said that trauma is "an intense experience that is stored in the body", no matter if it's something that the survivor themselves experienced or that they witnessed. There's both an emotional component and a physical component, which is something often overlooked when discussing a psychological trauma. This physical component is often something that is not released from the individual and goes with them. For example, some women who survive a sexual assault hold their trauma in their pelvis, causing constant pain and tension. Other people hold their trauma in their throat, perhaps because they were unable to scream during or speak up about their traumatic event. Other people hold it in their legs, other people hold it in their back – you get the gist. Oftentimes in trauma, that experience is not something that can be put into words, which is why the body stores it and shows symptoms of it, even if the mind doesn't recognize or understand what's going on. The body and the mind can almost become disconnected in this, and a common breakthrough experienced in the trauma healing process is the removal of that physical weight, which allows for the emotional release to follow.

Another key aspect of trauma is that the memories of the event are not encoded in your brain properly. Your brain can handle stressful things generally very well, such as the stress of finals week or the stress of a divorce. When the system gets so overloaded with sensory and emotional stimuli in a very short amount of time, though, the brain doesn't always cope so well. In these moments, some of those emotions and some of that energy that cannot be handled at the present moment are locked away, which contributes to the part of trauma that's stuck in the body. The brain also remembers those traumatic moments differently because of the overload occurring and the interactions of the neurohormones during that time. Cortisol, your body's main stress hormone, runs rampant during a trauma, but it's actually toxic to your hippocampus in large doses. Your hippocampus is involved in memory formation. Therefore, when your body secretes the large amount of cortisol that it does during a traumatic event, those hormones could be interfering with your hippocampus's ability to encode the memories from that situation properly. Reframing this incorrect memory process is a key part in some trauma therapies, such as eye movement desensitization and reprocessing (EMDR).

As we move forward, it's important for you to keep in

mind that every experience is individual. There's no "right" or "wrong" way to react to a potentially traumatic incident, no "right" or "wrong" way to hold your trauma, and no "right" or "wrong" way to heal from your trauma. You need to listen to yourself (and if you feel like you can't, then part of your healing will be to learn to listen to yourself again), recognize your boundaries, and follow what feels right to you through this journey. I and your future therapists are here to suggest, not to direct, as you are the sole individual in the driver's seat of your healing journey.

Are You a Victim, Survivor, Client, or Patient?

When discussing yourself after a trauma, it can be hard to figure out what to call yourself. Some consider themselves a victim, as something horrible has happened to them that's often out of their control. Some people will call themselves a survivor, as they've successfully made it through a traumatic event. Most mental health professionals use the term "client", though some hospitals and psychiatric units will use the term "patient". All of these different names have different connotations, so finding the right one to call yourself or to be called by a professional can be difficult, and that's the last thing you should be worrying about during your healing process.

The important thing to remember when discussing yourself is that – as I've said – there's no right way to do it! If you feel like a survivor, then by all means, call yourself a survivor! If you feel like a victim, then call yourself a victim! If you feel like a client…you get my point. Most mental health professionals, friends, and family members should and will follow your lead on this one, as the term you select for yourself is as unique to you as your experience with your trauma. You may already feel like you're being shoved in a box called "sexual assault", "lost a child", or whatever your traumatic incident contained, so there's absolutely no reason you should try to fit yourself in a different box if that title doesn't fit you.

Throughout this book, I'm going to use the term survivor, as changing from calling myself a victim to calling myself a survivor was a huge turning point in my healing process. I also find that it's simplest to stick with one term throughout a book instead of switching back and forth to try to please everyone who reads it. If you don't identify as a survivor, then please don't take offense or feel like this material is not applicable to you. I don't mean to exclude, ignore, or invalidate anyone with my terminology, so please feel free to mentally replace the word "survivor" with any word that you feel better suits you and your situation.

Trauma as a Public Health Crisis

When I spoke with Tracey Wilkins of the Willow Tree Healing Center in St. Paul, Minnesota, she stated that she believed that trauma was the largest public health crisis in the nation because it is the root of so many physiological and psychological health conditions. Barbara Nordstrom-Loeb, a dance-movement therapist from Minneapolis, Minnesota, agreed, especially when it pertains to psychiatric disorders. "Most of the diagnostic criteria [in the DSM] are the coping strategies, and if you go deeper, it's really trauma. All personality disorders – which never made sense to me when I studied it – are just people who don't have a sense of themselves. They never got that because of the situation around them growing up. This is just how they compensate for it and protect themselves. Anxiety, depression, eating disorders, addictions – all of that, in my experience, if you really take the time to go deep below the diagnosis, is trauma." While Tracey and Barbara's combined 54 years of professional experience is convincing, a revolutionary study by the CDC and Kaiser backed their claims.

This study examined the relationship of Adverse Childhood Experiences (ACEs) and adult health problems and came to a stunning conclusion: the more ACEs an individual underwent, the more health problems they had in adulthood. This is because those early ACEs, whether they were abuse, neglect, or family struggles, impaired neurodevelopment, which in turn impaired social, emotional, and cognitive functioning. This led to the adoption of health-risking behaviors and, subsequently, disease, disability, and social problems. This ultimately led to increased mortality rates and death at an earlier age.

Unfortunately, ACEs are common, as shown by the 2/3 of participants who reported one ACE and 1/5 of participants who reported three or more ACEs. These ACEs include emotional, sexual, or physical abuse; emotional or physical neglect; witnessing your mother being treated violently; substance abuse, criminal behavior, and/or mental illness in the household; or parental separation or divorce. As the number of

ACEs increases, the likelihood for developing a significant health concern or condition increases. These include, but are not limited to:

- Anxiety
- Asthma
- Autoimmune disease
- Broken bones
- Cancer
- Chronic pain
- COPD
- Depression and suicide attempts
- Diabetes
- Digestive problems
- Early death
- Early initiation of smoking and sexual activity
- Fetal death
- Financial stress, lower reported income, and unemployment
- Heart disease and heart attacks
- Headaches
- High blood pressure
- Intimate partner or sexual violence
- Liver and lung disease
- Multiple sexual partners and STDs
- Obesity
- Poor work performance and academic achievement (including work attendance and graduation rates)
- Stroke
- Substance use and abuse, including alcohol, illicit drugs, and nicotine (smoking)

- Unintended and adolescent pregnancies

How is this a public health crisis? Well, 2/3 of participants in the CDC-Kaiser study experienced an ACE, and over 17,300 people took part in that study. While it's never completely correct to say that the exact results and percentages found in a study apply to the entire population, it's widely accepted that a similar fraction of the general population has experienced an ACE, as well, because of the sheer number of participants in the original study. Furthermore, tens of studies have been completed about ACEs and their effects on adult health after the original CDC-Kaiser one with very similar results. Because of this, it's safe to say that a large percentage of the world has experienced at least one ACE in their life. Therefore, many individuals with the health concerns and conditions listed above may have said concerns and conditions because of (or partly because of) ACEs – because of childhood trauma. Trauma, as Tracey said, is "happening on a systemic level", and it's important to understand that when considering treatment options.

Because of the link between childhood trauma and adult health issues, trauma is also potentially the largest health-related economic crisis in the US. According to a study by Hall and Doran in 2016, the US spends approximately $170 billion per year on direct medical care for adults who smoke and loses $156 billion per year in lost productivity due to premature death and exposure to secondhand smoke. A 2015 study by Greenberg et al. showed that over $210 billion is spent each year in the US on Major Depressive Disorder, split evenly between medical costs and productivity losses.

Diabetes? $327 billion per year, according to the American Diabetes Association. Heart disease and stroke? $330 billion, plus 859,000 deaths per year. Excessive alcohol use? $249 billion. Cancer? Expected to reach $174 billion annually by 2020.

Now, I'm not saying that every person who has cancer has cancer because of an ACE, or that every person who drinks excessively does so because of trauma from their childhood. But let those numbers sink in for a little bit – even if only half of excessive alcohol drinkers drink because of an ACE, that's almost $125 billion per year that could be saved or redirected toward trauma treatment, prevention, and education. For those economists or epidemiologists out there, don't start coming at me for my rudimentary calculations. I am aware that I'm being idealistic – and frankly, unrealistic – by suggesting that the funds currently used for medical care are immediately and completely transferred to helping heal people's trauma. I'm not suggesting a magic cure to the financial setting of our healthcare system. I'm not even saying that it would be a quick, easy, or feasible fix. These numbers are just put out to get you to think about the mass effect that trauma has on the healthcare system and the economy. To repeat: my job and my purpose with this book are not to fix the country's trauma crisis; my job and my purpose are to help people on an individual level see other options for healing their trauma.

Chapter 3:
Trauma- and Stressor-Related Mental Health Disorders

⚘

I would feel remiss if I wrote a book about trauma but didn't include any information about the psychiatric diagnoses surrounding trauma, but I'm also hesitant to include this information. I just spent a whole chapter talking about how the responses to trauma are incredibly individual, and now I want to plop you in a diagnosis box! In my experience with trauma and mental health, I've found having a diagnosis both helpful and unhelpful. It's helpful because it gives me a bit of clinical understanding as to what's going on with me and reassures me that I'm not alone, as there are surely other individuals with the same diagnosis. On the other hand, it isn't helpful for me because I feel like my therapist zeroes in on the diagnosis and ignores the person and emotions surrounding it. Perhaps this was an issue with the therapist and not with the process of diagnosing in general, but it caused a lot of mental turmoil and debate surrounding diagnoses. I'm also not a huge fan of the word "disorder". While I'm aware that there's something out of sync in the brain when someone is diagnosed with a disorder, I feel like the word "disorder" makes the individual feel less-than or broken, neither of which are helpful in the healing process.

That being said, I recognize that not everyone thinks the same way that I do and that some people find diagnoses very helpful. I also need to recognize that there are individuals – maybe you – out there reading this book who have been diagnosed and want a better understanding of what they've been labeled with that doesn't include loads of technical jargon or a quick print-out that their therapist gave them. Whatever your reason is for reading this chapter on psychiatric diagnoses surrounding trauma, I hope it helps you understand what's going on psychiatrically a little bit more. At the very least, I hope it gives you a peek inside your therapist's head when they gave you this diagnosis. If you're someone who doesn't like diagnoses, then feel free to skip ahead.

If you choose to stay, then welcome to Trauma Disorders 101. You're probably thinking I'm about to talk about PTSD, which I am – but it's not the only psychiatric disorder surrounding trauma. The DSM-5 (the Diagnostic and Statistical Manual of Mental Disorders, 5th Edition) is the handbook for diagnoses for mental health practitioners, and it actually has a whole chapter titled Trauma- and Stressor-Related Disorders that discusses five disorders that can arise from trauma and stress. These disorders are similar in function to anxiety disorders, obsessive-compulsive disorders, and dissociative disorders. Many of them share similarities, but they are distinct in the medical field, so I'll make sure to highlight the important differences as I discuss them.

Reactive Attachment Disorder and Disinhibited Social Engagement Disorder

Reactive Attachment Disorder and Disinhibited Social Engagement Disorder are diagnoses given to children. Reactive Attachment Disorder appears in children aged 9 months to 5 years, and Disinhibited Social Engagement Disorder appears in children from 9 months to adolescence. Because of the audience of this book, I'm going to skip over the details of these two disorders, but if you're interested in learning more about them, check out a DSM from your local library or look up the information on the American Psychiatric Association's website.

Acute Stress Disorder

Acute Stress Disorder arises immediately after a traumatic event and lasts anywhere from three days to one month after the trauma. If it progresses past one month, it generally transitions into PTSD. In other words, it's a short-term stress response to a traumatic event. In order to be diagnosed with Acute Stress Disorder, you need to experience actual or threatened death, injury, or sexual assault. This experience can come from it happening to you, witnessing it, having it happen to a close friend or family member, or having repeated exposure to such events because of your job. Further diagnostic criteria include the presence of nine or more of the following symptoms:

- Distressing memories of the traumatic event
- Dreams that contain the trauma or themes related to it
- Flashbacks
- Psychological or physiological reactions or distress in response to internal or external scenarios that resemble the trauma
- Inability to experience positive emotions
- Altered sense of reality
- Dissociative amnesia or an inability to remember parts of the traumatic event
- Efforts to avoid memories or thoughts about the trauma
- Efforts to avoid physical objects, people, or places that remind you of the trauma
- Poor sleep
- Irritability and outbursts, often those that are aggressive, verbally or physically
- Hypervigilance
- Concentration problems
- Extreme startle response

In short, Acute Stress Disorder involves an anxiety response surrounding some form of re-experiencing your traumatic event. As the symptom list above describes, these re-experiences can be actual (meaning you see, hear, feel, smell, et cetera, something in real life that reminds you of the event) or psychological (meaning memories, dreams, and the like). An accompanying symptom of Acute Stress Disorder is strong negative emotions about yourself in relation to your trauma. For example, you could feel guilty about not preventing the trauma or feel incompetent because you didn't handle the trauma with more "mental fortitude". In addition, panic attacks, impulsivity, grief responses, and post-concussion symptoms are common in those with Acute Stress Disorder.

The rates of Acute Stress Disorder vary based on the type of trauma experienced. For example, less than 20% of individuals who experience a trauma develop Acute Stress Disorder, but only when that trauma isn't an interpersonal assault. When it is – things like rape or witnessing a mass shooting – the rates of Acute Stress Disorder can reach as high as 50%. Women and individuals who test high for neuroticism (one of the Big 5 personality traits) are also at higher risk for Acute Stress Disorder.

Adjustment Disorders

Adjustment Disorders are somewhat of a catch-all group that encompasses any emotional or behavioral symptom in response to a stressor that occurs within three months of the stressor. In order for you to meet the diagnostic criteria for an Adjustment Disorder, your distress needs to be above and beyond a normal grief response or above and beyond the expected normal for someone who experienced a trauma like yours (mm, normal – my favorite word in trauma healing. Take it with a grain of salt. They're talking about statistical averages of severity of symptoms, not societal norms or expectations.) and it needs to impact your day-to-day functioning. Adjustment Disorders are broken down into the following six subtypes:

- With depressed mood
- With anxiety
- With mixed anxiety and depressed mood
- With disturbance of conduct (how you act in society)
- With mixed disturbance of emotions and conduct
- Unspecified, meaning that your reactions warrant a diagnosis of an Adjustment Disorder, but they don't fit into one of the pre-established subtypes

Adjustment Disorders are also classified as acute, meaning that the symptoms last for less than six months after the completion of your trauma, or chronic, meaning the symptoms last for longer than six months.

Fitting in with the catch-all nature of Adjustment Disorders, the stressor or trauma that you experienced can be one event or multiple, recurrent or continuous, and affecting only you or a group of people. Adjustment Disorders are pretty common; 5-20% of outpatients are diagnosed with an Adjustment Disorder, and up to 50% of inpatients are, as well. Finally, Adjustment Disorders are often co-diagnosed with another mental disorder or physical illness, and it's often labeled as the psychological distress accompanying a physical diagnosis, such as cancer.

Posttraumatic Stress Disorder (PTSD)

Ah, the big one – PTSD. This is the most commonly thought of mental health disorder accompanying a traumatic event, likely because it gets the most media and entertainment attention. As with Acute Stress Disorder, those who are diagnosed with PTSD must have, in some way, experienced a traumatic event; the same definition of a traumatic event as with Acute Stress Disorder applies to PTSD, too. A combination of symptoms is required, as described below:

- At least one of the following intrusion symptoms:
  - Distressing memories of the traumatic event
  - Dreams that contain the trauma or themes related to it
  - Flashbacks
  - Psychological or physiological reactions or distress in response to internal or external scenarios that resemble the trauma
  - Efforts to avoid memories or thoughts about the trauma or physical objects, people, or places that remind you of the trauma
- Two or more of the following emotive and cognitive symptoms:
  - Dissociative amnesia or an inability to remember parts of the traumatic event
  - Persistent or exaggerated negative beliefs about yourself, the world, or the events surrounding your trauma
  - Distorted thoughts about the consequences of the trauma or your level of guilt in its

occurrence

- o Negative emotions, such as fear, horror, anger, guilt, or shame
- o Feeling disconnected or pulling away from others
- o Inability to experience positive emotions
- Two or more of the following behavioral symptoms:
  - o Poor sleep
  - o Irritability and outbursts, often those that are aggressive, verbally or physically
  - o Hypervigilance
  - o Concentration problems
  - o Extreme startle response
  - o Reckless or self-destructive behavior

As you can see, PTSD shares a lot of common symptoms with Acute Stress Disorder and, as I discussed in the description of Acute Stress Disorder, the timelines are very important in the differentiation of the two disorders. Acute Stress Disorder lasts for *at most* a month after the trauma, whereas PTSD cannot be diagnosed until the symptoms last *at least* one month after the trauma.

PTSD also has two subtypes: "with dissociative symptoms" and "with delayed expression". PTSD with delayed expression is diagnosed when the diagnostic criteria (the list of symptoms above) are not met until six months after the trauma. PTSD with dissociative symptoms is only diagnosed when the individual experiences consistent depersonalization (feeling like an outside observer of your body) or derealization (feeling like the world around you is distorted or a dream).

The prevalence of PTSD is relatively low; the lifetime risk of PTSD in the United States is only 8.7% at age 75, and it's even lower on other continents. Rates of PTSD are higher in individuals who have violent careers, such as military members or police officers, and the highest rates of PTSD are seen in survivors of rape, combat, internment, and genocide. As with Acute Stress Disorder, women are at higher risk for PTSD, and their symptoms generally last longer than males. That being said, approximately one half of adults are able to completely resolve their PTSD in three months with proper treatment, though that's definitely not to say that there aren't individuals who suffer from PTSD for years on end.

There's also a significant PTSD debate within the military community, as well, specifically around the word "disorder". I already expressed my beliefs about the word, and many members of the military believe labeling someone with a "disorder" makes them less likely to pursue help. They proposed that it be called an "injury", as that language is less damning and more in line with how members of the military speak. Members of the American Psychiatric Association believe that it's the culture of mental healthcare in the military, not the terminology used, that needs to change, and since they write the DSM, PTSD is staying a disorder for the foreseeable future.

What Does This Mean for Me?

As I discussed in the beginning of the chapter, I'm hesitant to include this information, and I'm definitely not qualified to tell you that you have a disorder or which one you have. This information is also not provided so that you can self-diagnose.

All I would encourage you to do with this information is see what feels right to you. Just because you haven't been diagnosed with a disorder does not mean that your symptoms, feelings, and struggles are not valid or do not warrant help; nothing could be further from the truth. On the other hand, just because you've been diagnosed with a trauma- or stressor-related disorder doesn't mean that your reactions are suddenly disproportionately more severe than others who didn't receive a diagnosis.

More specifically, there are strict requirements for what counts as a trauma for Acute Stress Disorder and PTSD. Instead of deciding what is a trauma by the level of emotions on the part of the survivor, the DSM created a list of what qualifies as a trauma. Sexual assault, for example, would meet the diagnostic criteria for PTSD, whereas an event that causes intense fear or helplessness would not. The reasoning behind this is that the level of emotion does not predict the onset of PTSD symptoms; instead, there are significant correlations between types of events and the onset of PTSD. After I spent so much time in the first chapter saying that a trauma is whatever is traumatic to you, this definition can come across as stifling or ignorant of the pain you went through and the level of healing you need now. Don't limit yourself to or define yourself by a diagnosis you receive or the information about the various disorders that I outlined above. Your trauma is yours. Your emotions are yours. Your healing is yours. Its severity is not defined or limited by a diagnosis.

Chapter 4:
Breakthroughs and Common Lessons Learned During Trauma Healing

ॐ

J ust as everyone's response to a traumatic incident is different, everyone's healing journey is different. Different methods of healing work for different people, and different people realize different things throughout their healing process. While everyone is individual, there are some common themes in the trauma healing process that are important for you to understand. These aren't as much checkmarks by which you can say that "yes, I'm done healing" or "no, I've still got a ways to go", but more reassurances that the feelings you're having during your healing process aren't odd, unusual, or wrong. It can also be helpful for you to understand some changes and revelations you might undergo during your healing process so that you can begin with the end in mind, so to speak, and feel a little less in the dark about the journey that's to come.

A Few Things to Remember, Spoken by Survivors Themselves

It's often completely unhelpful to hear random platitudes and comments from people who have no idea what you're going through, but the little tidbits I want to share with you have been spoken by survivors of trauma who contributed to this book by sharing their stories with me. In order to respect their privacy, I'm not going to share their names. While they may not have been in your exact shoes, they've been through their own traumatic experiences and stated that these lessons were things they learned through healing or things they wish they knew when they were healing.

"It's okay to not have all the answers."
Healing from trauma can be a confusing and scary experience. It takes facing something that has hurt you deeply and looking inside yourself to find answers that you might not want to find. During this whole process, you may feel like you need to know exactly what you're doing at all times and know exactly how you feel about everything that's going on, but that doesn't have to be the case. It's okay to allow yourself to learn and

heal at the same time. It's okay to admit that you don't know something. It's okay to be confused, scared, or any other emotion that you're feeling. Be gentle with yourself; healing isn't a perfect process.

"Trust yourself."

Your emotions and reactions are unique, but you and you alone are feeling them for a reason. Trust that what you're feeling is authentic to you and completely acceptable, and trust what your body and mind are telling you that you need to work through. Not every method, statement, or concept is going to work for everyone, and you'll know inside when something isn't right for you. Trust that. Trust that you know what you need, what you want, and what you're comfortable with. Let your body and your mind guide you through your healing.

"You'll be stronger because of it."

Healing from a trauma might be one of the hardest things you'll ever do, potentially second to surviving the trauma itself. Going through hard things makes you stronger – yes. Going through a hard thing that makes you pull apart yourself, give yourself grace, and trust yourself makes you stronger than you could ever imagine. While seeing that light at the end of the tunnel might seem futile, keep in the back of your mind that you're not going through this potentially painful healing process for nothing.

"Love yourself and accept your journey."

When you've experienced a trauma, it's not uncommon to turn

that hate, anger, and pain back onto yourself, and as you can probably guess, that's not very helpful in your healing journey. As hard as it might be to do, loving yourself and accepting your journey is going to make traveling that road to healing so much easier. If you're struggling to do that, take a moment to be proud of yourself for picking up this book. Many people try to push their trauma under the rug and live with the negative feelings, even if they're directed at themselves; you've decided that you're ready to turn over a new leaf in regards to your trauma, and that's something to be proud of. Sometimes all it takes is a little seed of pride or happiness to allow self-love and self-acceptance to enter you again. Even further, there's no right or wrong way to respond to a trauma or heal from it. There should be no self-judgement on your part because of how you're handling your healing journey. Don't compare yourself to others who have healed, and don't try to fit yourself on a healing timeline. Give yourself some grace.

"It can get worse before it gets better."

This is somewhat of a gross analogy, but think of a blister for a second. It's red, angry, and maybe a little visually unappealing, but when you pop it, a whole slew of gunk (very professional terms, I know) comes out. Then it scabs, maybe pops again, and takes a while to fully heal. The start of your trauma journey can be like interacting with a blister. You seem like you have it pretty well together on the outside, but when you start digging through your emotions around your traumatic experience, it can get messy, it can get painful, and it can seem like you're making backwards progress because everything

31

hurts so much again. In actuality, this is the only way to truly heal. If you keep slapping Band-Aid over Band-Aid on your traumatic experience, you're never going to wade through the mass of emotions surrounding it and learn how to manage them so that you can get back to living your life without that weight on you. Give yourself permission to hurt, to feel messy, and to dig through yourself as you start your healing process, because that's the only way to truly heal.

"Sometimes unexpected triggers pop up."
You've put the work into your healing process, everything's going well, then BAM – all of a sudden, something happens in your life and triggers a flashback, and you're sucked back down the trauma rabbit hole again. While it may feel like you've failed or that the work you put into your journey was all for naught, it's unfortunately completely normal. You can't prepare for every single possible trigger out there, but the difference between the triggers now and the triggers at the beginning of your healing journey is that you've learned some emotional regulation methods that you can put into place to reframe this new trigger, realize it's not catastrophic to your healing journey, and not allow it to drag you back down to where you started.

Even more importantly, recognize that healing from trauma is a stepwise process, especially with complex trauma (trauma that occurred over many instances and a long period of time). You can't address every single part of your trauma at once, so it's common for you to work on one part for a while, master that, then let it sit for a while. After some time, something else will pop up, and it's time to once again focus healing energy on your trauma, just this time on a different aspect of it. Oftentimes, the new parts that pop up occur with major life events, such as getting married or preparing to have kids. This is *not* a failure on your part or on the part of your healing methods. You just weren't at a place in life where you were able to process these new parts of your trauma, perhaps because you hadn't had the life experiences that triggered them yet or because you weren't at a developmental stage where you could process them. It's perfectly acceptable to roll with these new emotions surrounding your trauma and return to your healing journey so you can conquer them, just as you conquered the other pieces that you've already worked on.

For me, pieces of my trauma popped up when I figured out that I was not eligible for military service. My dream career was that of an Air Force Pararescueman, which is a mixture of a trauma paramedic and a search and rescue specialist. For those of you who are unfamiliar with the military enlistment process, part of the enlistment requirements is passing a medical exam, and the first part of that is a document that goes into every single aspect of your medical history. A history of self-harm is an automatic disqualification for any and all military service, and because I decided to tell the truth on that entry medical questionnaire, I was not eligible for military service. As funny as it sounds, I had to mourn the loss of that dream, and a lot of anger and resentment about my mental health history and my trauma popped up. Part of my career grieving process was dealing with those elements of my trauma that came up, and guess what – it was perfectly okay for me to do so.

"It's okay to spend more time with friends and family – even if that means going home."

For the longest time, I felt like going home after I left was a failure. I had carved out my own life for myself in different places all over the world, and I believed that crawling back to my little country home in Oregon would signify that I couldn't hack it out in the real world. What I learned, though, was that there's a form of healing in spending time with friends and family of your childhood, especially when you're recovering from something traumatic. When you're able to spend time with people who have known you for years – sometimes people who know you as well as you know yourself – and with people who are able to and want to care for you, it can take a load off your shoulders and allow you to spend a little more time taking care of you. It's not selfish, and it's not failure. After all, the only way that you can give 100% of yourself to that independent life you've created for yourself is if you have 100% to give, something that's darn near impossible to do when you're carrying around the aftereffects of a traumatic incident. Many trauma survivors have told me that they wished they spent more time with friends and family during their healing process, so if you have the chance to spend more time with loved ones, take it.

"Some changes might be permanent."

Just as a woman can't go through something as emotional as childbirth without being permanently changed, it's nearly impossible for you to experience something traumatic and not be changed, too. Now, this doesn't mean that you'll constantly experience flashbacks or other symptoms of your post-traumatic stress; actually, these changes can be positive. I won't go into extreme detail here because I cover all this in the chapter about what happens after healing, but realize that it's possible to incorporate the puzzle piece of your trauma into your life's puzzle and use that to positively impact those around you. Recognizing that your trauma can be a gift instead of or in addition to a burden is a huge milestone in your healing process.

Many People Feel a Weight Lifted from Their Body

As I talked about when defining trauma, every psychological trauma has an emotional and physical part. This physical part often manifests in a certain part of your body, and during the healing process, many individuals describe feeling like a weight is lifted from them. This is the physical residue from the trauma leaving your body, and this makes way for the emotional side of the trauma to leave, as well. The movement of certain therapeutic methods that I'll cover, whether that be through dance-movement therapy or the movement involved with equine-assisted therapy, helps release this physical aspect of trauma. This then allows for a peace to overcome you.

You'll See Your Trauma from a New Perspective

Before you start your healing process, it's common for

you to only see your trauma through one lens, and furthermore, to only react to triggers in one way. Through these healing methods, it's common for people to gain a new perspective on their traumatic experience. Before, there was only one way to view it and react to it, whereas, now, there are multiple ways. This allows for a different reaction to triggers. Instead of barreling down the same response as before, you'll be able to recognize what's happening, breathe through it, and respond instead of react.

You Are Worthy of a Place in This World

In many traumatic situations, survivors take the pain, anger, and negative feelings that they have toward their attacker, abuser, or the cause of their trauma and turn it toward themselves. This is particularly true with child abuse survivors, where, instead of hating their abuser, they hate themselves. This can manifest in anything from self-harm to eating disorders and more, and it's common for trauma survivors to feel an "inability to value themselves", as Sally, the chief development officer of Acres for Life, put it. Sometimes this stems from a feeling of being marred by their trauma, and other times it stems from feeling like they're at fault for the event. Other times it's impossible to put into words why that feeling of loathing was turned on themselves. If you're feeling this way, or anything similar to it, have hope, as a common breakthrough for individuals healing from trauma is the understanding that not only do they have a place in the world, but that they deserve one.

You Develop Your Identity

The very first way that we learn about ourselves and begin to develop an identity is through the interactions of bodies. We learn that we have a body, and other people have a body, and our bodies interact in various ways. Unfortunately, during trauma, that standard interaction of bodies can be violently disrupted, thereby causing a disruption in your sense of self, as well. When many people begin to heal from trauma and start to believe that their body is a safe place again, they often get curious about their body and its place in the world, which can lead to profound levels of identity development.

At a very base level, you'll learn that you have a body and that you hold a place in the world. You'll learn that you have wants and needs, and that it's okay to have them. You'll learn that you can have healthy boundaries, assert yourself, and choose who enters your life and occupies the space around you. These are very common cultural values and are critical for understanding your identity and place in society.

The Trauma Wasn't Your Fault

As I just discussed, many individuals feel like they're at fault for the trauma. While I can understand how that happens because of the maelstrom of emotions regarding the event, it's important for you to know that it was not your fault. No sexual abuse survivor "asks for it" by dressing a certain way. No domestic violence survivor "deserved it" because of a housekeeping error. Unfortunately, bad things happen to good people, people who didn't ask for it, *people who are not at fault*, and the best thing that you can do for yourself and your life moving forward is work to regain a sense of control and normalcy, partly through recognizing that you are not at fault for what happened to you.

Let's say, though, that you were texting and driving and got into a horrible and traumatic car accident. Some may say that it was your fault because you were on your phone. While you might be responsible for the events that occurred, your trauma is no less valid and no less worthy of healing than, say, a sexual assault survivor. Frankly, I don't believe in fault and blame. They don't achieve anything in life; the energy that you're using to blame yourself could be much better spent on healing yourself. Getting stuck in a tunnel of blame helps no one, including yourself.

Chapter 5:
Support Groups, Religion, and the Role of Friends and Family

⚉

W hen considering healing from trauma, it's critical to understand the role that your family and friends play, both those in your present life and those from your childhood. "Someone who's had a fairly safe upbringing, safe people, and safe experiences can have really hard, scary things happen to them and it's easier to come back to something more normal," Barbara, our aforementioned dance-movement therapist, explained. This has everything to do with the safe and healthy upbringing they had that taught them how to cope effectively and how to maintain stable mental states. For some people, though, their trauma starts at birth.

"Some of them had surgery right after they were born. I always imagine this infant that's just been born, and it's cold and light, and somebody's cutting you open. You don't have the part of your brain [you need] to make any sense of it," Barbara explained. Because of early childhood trauma and your attachment strength growing up, healing from trauma varies greatly depending on how many layers of trauma and positive attachment there are.

The people currently in your life are just as important, too. Are you currently in a supportive environment, or are you in one where trauma is the norm, and therefore you might not even realize that you're traumatized? If you are coming from a broken system, whether that be a literal legal system, an unhealthy relationship, or something else entirely, participating in a healthy healing procedure and then returning back to that broken system will make change incredibly difficult. Your newfound strength and empowerment can sometimes be threatening in unhealthy home environments or relationships, and those people can try to strip it from you.

It sounds dramatic, but Lynn, the co-founder and CEO of Acres for Life, an equine-assisted therapy center in Minnesota, explained that the importance of the home environment is the "million-dollar question". That's why, at Acres for Life and in many other therapeutic environments, the discussion about including the family or significant other starts early in the process. It's not uncommon to bring one of those individuals – even if it's just one of many siblings – to a session to try to mend that relationship as soon as possible in the healing process. "A healthy horse needs a healthy herd," as Sally said;

in other words, you need a healthy support system in order to become healthy yourself. If members of your family or certain friends that you have are not supportive, then simply don't use them as a support system. Silence is an answer, so if you don't want to respond to their attempts to "help" or their attempts to stifle your healing process, you can absolutely take space and remove yourself from that situation. You're an adult – you don't owe them anything.

I don't mean to damn any and all family members in your life, though. Some can be incredibly beneficial to your healing process, and if you have a supportive relationship with someone, then utilize it. Healing from trauma is not an easy process, so using all the resources that are available to you is not only smart, but also necessary. Don't allow any expectations that a strong person wouldn't rely on friends or family for help prevent you from asking for help from supportive people in your life, and don't feel weak for leaning on them. The most important thing, though, when considering using friends or family members as support systems in your trauma healing process, is to ensure that you know what is and isn't safe for you and to ensure that you have proper boundaries set up for interactions with that friend or family member. For example, though they could be well-meaning, their pushiness for you to open up could be detrimental to your healing process if you're not ready to open up yet, so it's imperative that you know your boundaries and what you're comfortable with. Your healing journey is more important than their desire to know what happened.

It's your job to articulate to that friend or family

member how their "support" is affecting you if you want that relationship to be a supportive and healthy one. Hilary Mueller, a therapist and trauma-sensitive yoga practitioner from St. Paul Minnesota, said, "You can have a bunch of people in your life who love you and care about you, and none of those people are supportive because they don't know how to be." There are a few ways that you can serve as the educator for your friend or family member. The first way is to hand them this book and point them to the last, bonus chapter at the end of the book that helps people understand how to properly help someone healing from trauma. You may need to add some specifics about what works and doesn't work for you as an individual, but the final chapter is a great place to start. The second and third ways involve working with your therapist: you can either bring your friend or family member into session and work it out together, as I said above in regards to Acres for Life's therapy process, or you can get some homework from your therapist and talk it out with your friend or family member at home. Though it's critical to your healing process to have a safe home environment, don't feel rushed to bring someone who desperately wants to be a support system for you into session. Hilary told me a story of a client she was working with who took two years of therapy to consider telling her family that she was a survivor of trauma, and there was absolutely nothing wrong with that client's timeline.

Unfortunately, involving friends or family members in your trauma healing journey can incur sort of a 'damned if you do, damned if you don't' mentality if they aren't supporting you in a way that helps you. By this, I mean that individuals will treat you and interact with you based on the manner in which you appear and what they know about you. "If you're reclusive or you avoid things and keep [your trauma] to yourself, [people could think that] you're antisocial, you don't care about anybody else, you're selfish, and that is also traumatizing," Hilary explained. "If you tell the world, they might view you as 'you deserved it' or as fragile." Obviously, neither of those reactions from loved ones is helpful or healthy, which is why it's so important that they know how to help you. The final chapter of this book is a great resource for people trying to support you and who want to do it in the best way possible.

It's also important to note that having someone support you doesn't mean that they know every part of what happened to you during your traumatic event. Rather, they need to know how to help you, as I hammered in above. "I don't know that it's a necessary part of healing to rehash trauma events," Hilary said. "There are ways to heal from trauma that are not traumatizing," and going over and over every detail of your trauma to every single individual who wants to support you can be retraumatizing (and frankly exhausting). Barbara agreed with this sentiment: "Sometimes knowing the story of the trauma actually gets in the way." Again, silence is an answer, and you don't owe them your whole story just because they're trying to help you.

Benefits of Religion

As with the involvement of friends and family members, the general rule of thumb for religion and religious groups is "if it's helpful, keep it". Religious groups often provide a sense of community, which is critical in maintaining overall health and well-being. One trauma survivor, who lost her father when she was a young child, found that believing that God is in control, even if it doesn't make sense, was very helpful for her, as was her mom's encouragement to pursue her faith. When she lost her boyfriend to a motorcycle accident her senior year of college, she found that attending church for the community and the chance to meet guys her age helped her healing, as well.

On the other hand, religion and religious groups can sometimes mimic abusive environments because of their controlling and regulated nature and the expectations that are placed on their members. I'm not saying that every religious group is like this, but I'm also not saying that a religious group has to reach cult-hood before it carries these characteristics. I went to Catholic high school, and though I was not Catholic, I attended monthly mass with the rest of the student population. There were many of my classmates who were highly devout, and when I asked them why they did certain rituals during the mass, their response was that they did it because the Father or another religious official told them to. Why they took communion? Because they were told to. Why they went through Confirmation? Because they were told to.

Beyond the practice of following directions, there were high expectations that you would follow them. I didn't want to stand up and walk through the communion line because I wasn't Catholic, yet I was not allowed to simply stay in my seat while the Catholic students went up to receive communion. I definitely wouldn't say that my high school religious environment or the Catholic church is uniformly abusive, but I would firmly state that the regulations and expectations of practicing Catholicism can *mimic* the regulations and expectations of abusive relationships, which can be extremely unhealthy and feel very unsafe for individuals recovering from a trauma, particularly one that took place because of an abusive environment.

Overall, religious groups can be very helpful for some individuals who have a strong conviction in their faith, but they can be very stifling and triggering for others who don't gain the same sense of community and belonging from religion. It's up to you to see how you feel in those environments and decide to participate or not accordingly. It's also important to note that going to church is not the equivalent of therapy, and it should not be thought of as the sole healing method in your journey. It can be a great support system and additive to your healing journey, but it's important to work with a therapist, perhaps through one of the methods later discussed, as well.

Benefits of Support Groups

The golden rule of social interactions when healing from trauma applies to support groups, as well. Oftentimes, support groups are a temporary help. In the beginning, it can provide a sense of community and be beneficial talking to people who understand the devastating effects of trauma. Furthermore, Carol Polacek, a psychologist from Syracuse, New

York, says that "support groups help [trauma survivors] learn skills to manage their emotional reactions and behaviors. They learn how the trauma affects them, their emotions, feelings, behaviors, and brain pathways." After a while, though, it can start to become detrimental after you've shared your story over and over. You start to spin your wheels a little bit, and if this happens to you, it's time to move on to a different healing method or supportive environment.

When you enter a support group, it's important for you to listen to yourself and your body regarding what feels safe, and an easy way to do that is to ask yourself some questions: Does it feel safe to be in this room? Does it feel safe to go, but maybe not share until next time, when I feel better about it? Questions like this help you feel out a situation that might or might not be helpful for you, and listening to the answers you receive helps you make decisions that are the best for you and your healing journey.

If you're interested in participating in or trying out a support group, there are a few ways to go about finding one. While it's worth putting some time looking at local churches, non-profits, and other organizations to see if they offer any support groups, Psychology Today has a great resource at www.psychologytoday.com/us/groups/trauma-and-ptsd. You can enter your location and find support groups in your area. You can also filter this list by the gender of the support group host and the age to which the group caters. If you're located outside of the US, you can change your country by the drop-down menu in the upper-righthand corner of the screen. At the time of writing, this searching tool works in multiple countries.

The Best Social Support for Trauma Healing

The most important aspect of your social interactions when healing from trauma is to find a place where you feel connected, supported, and loved. This could be your friends and family, a church system, a support group, or even something as innocuous as a book club. You don't have to open up to these individuals, but you can if you want to. In other words, listen to yourself and recognize whether you want to talk about your journey or simply relax and enjoy a fun activity. The support systems in your life should be willing to follow your lead.

Chapter 6:
Introduction to Healing

⚛

Everyone's healing journey is completely unique to them. No one method is going to work for everyone, and some individuals might find varying levels of efficacy from the same healing method. If you've picked up this book, you're likely either in one of two mindsets towards trauma healing methods. Option A is that you're just starting out your healing process and want to pursue natural, integrative, and holistic methods first. That's fantastic! This entire section will walk you through a variety of such healing methods.

Option B – the other way you're likely approaching your healing journey – is that you've had a negative experience with traditional counseling methods, so you're ready to pursue other healing methods that don't have you lying on the proverbial therapist's couch twice a week for an hour. I've had many trauma survivors tell me that they found that traditional counseling methods didn't work for them or that they found that receiving an official diagnosis – such as PTSD – was detrimental to their healing process. I experienced a similar thing myself. When you consider the fact that trauma affects your whole body, it makes sense that traditional talk therapy methods, such as Cognitive Behavioral Therapy (CBT), don't always work on their own. "Part of the challenge of the more cognitive-based approach with trauma is that when someone is triggered or when they're traumatized, they're not in the part of the brain that's functioning during cognitive therapeutic approaches," described Barbara. CBT addresses the mind and the cognitive processes in the prefrontal cortex, whereas trauma affects the limbic system in the brain and the entire body. While CBT has its place and can be a key part to a successful healing journey, it's not uncommon to find that it alone is not sufficient to help you heal.

In this book, I'm not going to give you a diagnosis. I'm not going to tell you that the only way to truly heal is to complete traditional counseling methods. That's neither my role here nor something that I am qualified to do. I'm merely here to show you alternative ways that you can accomplish the same goal of healing from your trauma. How you choose to do that – traditional or otherwise – is up to you, but I hope that these next few chapters can open your eyes to all the roads you can go down in your healing journey. The methods that I'm going to share with you are intuitive, as they tie into our primitive roots as humans – being around animals, being outside, and moving. While these concepts seem so simple, I and some others believe that these links make these therapies so effective because they touch our deepest and oldest selves, a level that trauma, too, touches. Sure, they're less common than traditional talk therapies, and yeah, they might have less FDA-approval supporting them, but the tides are turning to therapeutic methods like these, and doors to natural and integrative therapies are opening for you at a rate they never have before.

That being said, in a world that has been dominated by science and proof for so long, letting go of some of those rigid explanations and simply trusting that something works can be challenging. Yes, understanding the science of healing can be helpful, but recognizing the feeling of healing is, in my opinion, what matters most in the end. If you disagree, though, let me ask you this: why do we have faith if it can't be proven? Billions of people around the world believe in some form of a god or gods, yet no one can prove the existence of one. That doesn't stop them from gathering weekly or daily to celebrate their deity, praying to that deity, and believing that their deity carries them and protects them through this crazy ride called life. Some of these therapies are the same. Just as we can't prove that a god exists, we can't break down the healing powers of nature into a scientific formula, nor do we understand exactly what goes on in the brain that makes eye-movement desensitization and reprocessing so effective. If you are only willing to work with a therapy method that has decades of empirical research supporting it, I can't stop you. I only ask that, if you find that those methods don't work, you try something from this book and have faith in your own experience, instead of a lab report or an FDA label.

A Cautionary Word

Over the next few chapters, as I said, I'll explore and explain various methods of healing from trauma that are natural, integrative, holistic, and, in some cases, methods that you can do at home, on your own. With this, though, comes a cautionary word, as the presence and guidance of a mental health professional is not only helpful but occasionally necessary for safety. The role of a mental health professional in therapies like these is more of a facilitator than a leader; they are there to help you explore yourself and find your boundaries, but most of all, listen to yourself and let you guide the experience. They are not there to judge you, criticize you, or tell you what to do or how to feel, and they're not there to make you feel like you're being controlled.

This level of guidance and awareness of your limits is not something that just anyone, including yourself, is trained in. The leader of your local meditation group or the individual who runs a dance group for people healing from trauma likely isn't able to recognize when a meditative experience turns into a dissociative episode or when a crazy dance session turns into a psychotic break (both of these scenarios actually happened to individuals that Barbara worked with).

For some people, calming down and relaxing makes the world feel unsafe, and they're not ready to let down their guard. For others, expressing so much emotion and energy through a dance session allows their feelings and body to run completely out of control. The goal – or at least, one of them – of most trauma therapies is to help you understand that the world is a safe enough place to exist calmly in, and when you're allowed to delve into yourself, move your body, or otherwise interact with your trauma in ways that are unsupervised and lead to a lack of control or too much emotive expression, that sense of safety and control can be jeopardized.

That's not to say that the at-home methods discussed here, like meditation and nature exposure, are dangerous and unhelpful; it's quite the opposite. They are incredibly beneficial for certain individuals, and if you're currently experiencing great success with something you're doing on your own, then, by all means, keep doing it. This is just a word of advice that not everyone is able to heal on their own, nor should everyone try to. For your own safety and the most effective healing journey, seek the guidance of a mental health professional alongside your at-home methods of healing.

If you're hesitant about working with a mental health professional, please first know that you're understood. I felt like it was ridiculous to open up to and trust a complete stranger when I first started seeing a therapist, and the mental health professionals themselves understand your reservations (I've now built a great relationship with my current therapist, but that sense of distrust was there at the beginning for sure). Recognize that they are there to help you when you need them and that their role is to follow you and let your story come out naturally; they're not there to force it out of you. Also, really understand the model of healing that you're undergoing and understand why you think it would work for you. Each of the methods I'll discuss are founded in different things, whether that be horses, nature, movement, or something else entirely. One will likely appeal to you more than others, so get a good understanding of that method before you practice it. I'll do my best to give you an overview here, but ask questions of your mental health professional and share your reservations if you're uncertain about something in the process.

Chapter 7:
Eye Movement Desensitization and Reprocessing (EMDR)

ભ

I f you've heard of EMDR but don't know much about it beyond the fact that the therapist waves their hand in front of your face a bunch of times, then join the club. I had no idea what this therapy was when I started researching alternative methods for trauma healing, but after multiple trauma survivors that I spoke to told me how helpful it was in their healing process, I knew I needed to look into it more and include in it my list of options for you. If you're skeptical, no worries. Tracey Wilkins, the woman who introduced me to the concept of trauma as a public health crisis and a licensed EMDR practitioner, was "an absolute skeptic" when she first heard about EMDR, too. "It's a treatment that, 20 years ago, I thought was bologna," Tracey said. "I thought, 'How could anyone ever heal from *that*?'" Over time, though, as Tracey started delving more into trauma treatment, she recognized that big names in trauma treatment across the country (as well as personal colleagues and friends) were attesting to the power of EMDR. After doing her own research, she attended an EMDR training and became a licensed practitioner. "It really has changed some people's lives that I wouldn't have been able to help in the same way otherwise," Tracey added. Through the research I've done and the testimonials of Tracey and many trauma survivors, I've been convinced of the power of EMDR for trauma healing, too.

Before I go into the steps of EMDR and exactly how it works, I want to share some of the benefits and some of the incredible success stories of individuals who have been helped by EMDR. Tracey told me a few stories of her clients who achieved immense levels of healing with EMDR, starting with a woman who had four trauma memories that needed to be re-processed. She was highly anxious, never letting her children do anything without checking in and always carrying her pepper spray with her because she saw someone around every corner (side note about pepper spray: as a women's self-defense instructor, I think pepper spray and mace are great things. I highly recommend carrying it with you as a protective measure when you're out and about. I even recommend getting a second container and practicing on an unsuspecting tree so you know how it works! Pepper spray is a great protective measure, but it becomes unhealthy when you carry it because you are absolutely terrified of everyone and everything in the world.). By the time that this woman was done reprocessing her first memory, she had loaned her pepper spray to her friend and was able to walk her dog without the anxiety of not having her pepper spray. After all of her memories were reprocessed, she had taken a solo trip to Europe, took a trip with her daughter to Jamaica, and allowed her son to go on a school trip to Washington DC (and didn't chaperone him). EMDR didn't remove from her all of her caution and street smarts, but it did remove her crippling anxiety about living daily life.

Another client came to Tracey because she started having complete breakdowns after she dropped her daughter off at college for the first time. She couldn't work, couldn't get out of bed, and couldn't stop crying. It turned out that she had been raped twice, once in college and once just after, and had survived early childhood trauma. Sending her daughter to college caused her brain and body to bring these memories back up. After reprocessing the memories of the childhood trauma, she was able to have a decent relationship with her father for the first time in her adult life, and after reprocessing the two sexual assaults, she was able to go back to work and stopped having issues with depression and anxiety. Her personal and sexual relationship with her husband flourished, too, and all of this is thanks to EMDR.

What is EMDR?

EMDR works to reframe how you view yourself and the traumatic event you went through. If you've heard of

EMDR before, you've probably heard that the therapist sits in front of you and waves their hand back and forth in front of your face like a metronome, and all of a sudden your traumatic events don't feel so traumatic anymore. While that's the *very* basic gist of it, there's actually an eight-step process to EMDR, and the bilateral hand movement is only a piece of it. The first two steps involve taking the client history and explaining the process of EMDR. Then, the third step invites the client to visualize an image of the traumatic event, including the actual event, the emotional and physical sensations surrounding the event, and the client's negative self-perception because of the event. "This could be anything, like 'I'm worthless' or 'I don't feel safe anywhere'," Tracey explained. The client is also asked to imagine what they would like to believe about themselves when thinking about the traumatic event. For example, this could change their belief about being worthless to a belief that they are a valuable human being. Step three concludes with the client rating their distress from zero to 10 and the strength of the positive belief from zero to seven. Many times, clients will start their EMDR treatment process at an eight, nine, or 10 on the distress scale, and the goal is to get them down to a zero by the end of the treatment. Similarly, many clients will start at a zero on the positive belief scale, and an additional goal of EMDR is to get them to a seven.

Step four is when the reprocessing with the bilateral movement actually begins. This is what most people think of when they think of EMDR. The therapist will move their hand back and forth in front of the client, crossing the client's center plane and thus stimulating both sides of the brain. The hand will move "fast enough that it's a little bit challenging for people to keep up with", according to Tracey, but your eyes won't be a supersonic ping-pong ball for the entirety of the session. After the traumatic incident is reframed, step five comes into play, which is imprinting the positive belief. "There are two ways to do bilateral stimulation," Tracey explained. "The really fast way is to process. The slow way is to put things in." When it's time to imprint the positive belief into your mind, your therapist will slow down the rate of the bilateral movement to switch the effect that it has on your brain.

Steps six, seven, and eight are the conclusion of an EMDR session. Step six instructs the client to scan their body and look for any remaining tension or negative emotion from the original traumatic event. Step seven is the therapist explaining what to expect and how to handle things that pop up between sessions, and step eight is the process of checking in and potentially repeating the process during subsequent sessions.

The EMDR process breaks down the sum total of your trauma into individual memories, and, therefore, it's difficult to say how long reprocessing your whole trauma will take. "Some memories can be done in one session," Tracey said. "If it's a substantial trauma event, one memory could take three or four sessions." Many people have complex trauma, so it's usually not a one-and-done therapy. Sometimes, the process can be lengthened because a particular memory is a sticking point for you. If that's the case, you and your therapist will figure out a way to work through or around that memory so that you can successfully reprocess it and move on to tackle other memories of your trauma. One way to do this is to change the speed or direction of the hand movement. It can be sped up a bit, slowed down a bit, or changed to move on a diagonal. This causes the brain to perk up because of the break in routine, and that can be helpful for moving past a particularly challenging memory.

There are some books out there that teach you how to administer EMDR on yourself, but I wouldn't recommend trying to practice EMDR at home because you really have no clue what's going to come up. It might be okay and you might be able to handle it, sure, but I highly advise that you work with a licensed mental health professional so they can help carry you through the healing process. Furthermore, make sure that you're working with someone who's gone through a full EMDR training as opposed to someone who read a little bit about it and thinks they can administer it successfully.

The only piece of EMDR that can be done safely without a trained therapist is the affirmation of the positive belief. Some therapists will send their clients home to perform slow bilateral stimulation – the kind that imprints thoughts instead of reprocesses them – on themselves while holding on to the positive belief about themselves. This at-home bilateral stimulation is not waving your hand in front of your face; it would most likely be something like tapping on your legs, but that will depend on your therapist. That being said, don't take these last three sentences and think that you can self-administer EMDR. The at-home piece would be under the instruction of a trained practitioner and only after you've started and undergone some therapy with them.

Why Does EMDR Work?

I told you – a little skeptical, right? How can moving a hand back and forth in front of your face change how you view your trauma and yourself? It actually has a lot to do with REM (Rapid Eye Movement) sleep. Our body has natural mechanisms for handling emotionally traumatic events, and REM sleep is usually when this healing occurs. The eye movements during EMDR resemble the eye movements during REM sleep, thus allowing the body to tap into that healing mechanism. "The idea is that, by engaging both sides of your brain through this bilateral stimulation – which is the eye movement back and forth – we think that that's allowing your brain to reprocess this material. What happens, then, is it can encode properly," Tracey explained. When the memories are able to be encoded properly, it neutralizes the potency of the past traumatic event and allows it to be recalled without all the pain and emotions surrounding it. EMDR also allows the client to imprint a more positive image of themselves onto the memory, thereby improving stress levels and self-confidence.

It's all fine and dandy to talk about encoding memories properly, but it can be a bit difficult to understand what that means for you. Let's take the example of a car accident. If you've ever been in a car accident, you know how scary and frightening that can be. Your heart was likely pounding, your breathing rate increased, and you might have been a bit shaky. When you look back on that memory, though, your heart doesn't start pounding, your breathing rate doesn't increase, and you don't start shaking. That's a properly encoded memory. You can remember the feelings and remember the situation, but you don't become overwhelmed by those emotions and sensations when you merely recall the memory. With incorrectly coded events, though, such as trauma, that's not the case. "We have the memory and, along with that, we have all of the emotional stuff," Tracey said. "Sometimes it can feel like it's happening again in this very moment." In those triggering moments or flashbacks, it can be hard for your brain to tell the difference between living it and remembering it, and a goal of EMDR is to eliminate the emotional response to remembering the event by recoding the memory.

Unfortunately, not much is known about the neurobiological happenings that take place during EMDR. The exact manner in which it jump-starts that self-healing mechanism or the exact manner of that self-healing system is unknown. That being said, SPECT scans (scans that produce a 3D image of the brain using gamma rays) have shown neurological differences in activation in the brain when thinking about a traumatic experience before and after EMDR, so it's been scientifically proven that EMDR has an observable effect on the brain. How it creates that effect, though, has yet to be concretely discovered.

Where to Find an EMDR Therapist

Any EMDR practitioner who is worth their salt will be certified under the EMDR International Association (EMDRIA), and they have a searchable database where you can find licensed practitioners. This database can be accessed at www.emdria.org/find-a-therapist/. Here, you can search for EMDR therapists by radius from your home location or by the therapist's name (perhaps because you're looking to verify that someone is actually trained). EMDR therapists are pretty common (there were 49 of them within 10 miles of my zip code), so you should be able to find one that's close to home and easily accessible for you.

Chapter 8:
Craniosacral Therapy

◖◗

C raniosacral therapy (CST) is a method of healing that involves the practitioner laying their hands on your body, feeling the mobility of various areas of your body and the vibrations of the cerebrospinal fluid in your brain and spinal cord, and harnessing the body's natural healing methods – the same healing methods that constantly regenerate your body's cells, fight off pathogens, and heal everyday bumps and bruises – to release your stored trauma. In regards to trauma, craniosacral therapy addresses the physical aspect of it more than the emotional. "It's not necessarily that we'll do a lot of talking about [the emotions]; we'll just acknowledge it and go more into the [physical] sensation that comes up," Kate Mackinnon, a craniosacral therapy practitioner from Livermore, California, said. "It's as if the mind knows the story and has processed it and comes to terms with it and figured it out, but the physical in the tissue has not. It's almost like their somatic story has been left behind." This "somatic story" is the stuck energy leftover from a trauma.

Where does that energy come from? During a traumatic event, a key characteristic – regardless of the type of trauma – is a systemic overwhelm. There is too much emotion coursing through too quickly for someone to process, so the energy and emotions that cannot be processed or handled appropriately at the time become areas of stored energy in the body. That stuck energy can create tension, which in turn can pinch and distort the spinal column and the spinal cord within it.

The areas of stuck energy are identified through the laying-on of the hands of the practitioner and searching for the craniosacral rhythm, which is a rolling sensation in response to the volume change of the cerebrospinal fluid, the fluid that surrounds the brain and spinal cord. This rhythm reflects how the body is doing; in areas where the body is struggling, the amplitude of the rhythm will weaken. "I'll use a technique where we can feel into where the energy is being held and where it is being walled off in the body," Kate explained. "I'll also tug in through the fascia – where is it accommodating and where is it being caught up?" The fascia is the connective tissue that runs throughout the body, and it can tell the practitioner key information about where trauma is being held. In an ideal situation, the practitioner's hands would glide over the body, but when trauma is stuck in an area of fascia, the practitioner's hands would feel a "tug", or get caught up.

When the craniosacral therapy practitioner identifies areas of tension in the body, he or she will focus their hands on that area, adding about five grams of pressure to mirror the pressure that the body is exerting. This allows you to realize information about the inner workings of your body that you might not have known before and have a deeper connection with your body, something that many trauma survivors struggle with. It's also important to know that the areas of your body that are determined through craniosacral therapy as areas that hold trauma are not always the areas in which you feel pain.

The goal of craniosacral therapy is to activate the body's self-healing mechanisms. These mechanisms are happening constantly, as shown by your body's never-ending repairing and replacing of cells or your body's ability to heal a flesh wound. Craniosacral therapy accesses that mechanism, amplifies it, and supports it, either through providing external resources or energetically supporting it during the session. "A lot of times, in terms of trauma, people need to feel safe and they need to have trust established," Kate said. "You're creating a container that will hold the experience of looking at what happened." The container that's created during craniosacral therapy often focuses on the wisdom, skills, and resources that you've gained in the time since your trauma and using them as a lens for viewing your trauma. When you're able to view and release that trauma from your body, the craniosacral therapy practitioner might place their hands on the area that's holding the trauma and ask you to describe what you're feeling. Oftentimes, the releasing of trauma is warm or described as a heat, though for some complex traumas, it can feel cold, like your body is "defrosting" from the trauma.

Many people turn to craniosacral therapy as a last

resort. They've been down many other roads, and still feel like something is missing or that there's a more holistic approach available than their current conglomeration of medications and therapies. While craniosacral therapy can serve as that additional pathway to healing, it's ideal that craniosacral therapy is conducted in conjunction with other forms of healing. A craniosacral therapy practitioner can take the primary role in that team of healers and their healing methods, or they can support another primary form of therapy. For example, while craniosacral therapy does address some emotional aspects that come up during the session, Kate says that she would bring in the help of a certified therapist if there was significant emotional material surfacing during the craniosacral therapy sessions. Other common members of a healing team include acupuncturists, spiritual counselors, and bioenergeticists.

Another aspect of craniosacral therapy that's important for considerers to know is that it's incredibly client-led. Craniosacral therapy is all about "listening to the inner wisdom and inner knowing of the body," as Kate described; it's not about forcing your body to align itself in a certain way. If, for example, you have an area of stuck energy that needs to move one way or another, you have the ability to move your body how you feel you need to, and the practitioner will follow. You also have the ability to recognize that the practitioner's touch doesn't feel good and ask them to remove their hands or move them to a different area. This is incredibly important, especially since craniosacral therapy involves somewhat intimate contact with a relative stranger.

Alongside this client-led nature, though, comes an

important aspect of self-responsibility. In Kate's words, "you're really showing up for yourself. You're the leader. You're in charge." You'll really start to listen to your body and to things that have been tucked away for a very long time, and that can be painful. It can be easy to place your healing solely on the shoulders of your practitioner, but it's just as much your responsibility to discover and determine what your path to healing will look like.

Dolphin-Assisted Craniosacral Therapy

Dr. John Upledger, the creator of craniosacral therapy, was practicing craniosacral therapy in Florida and noticed that the dolphins would circle around the therapy that was occurring. The dolphins would often visit the practitioner first, but they'd also place their nose on areas of pain or stuck energy on the recipients of the craniosacral therapy. The dolphins would continue to work with the client, either through clicking, touching, or making waves in the water, and Dr. Upledger found that the involvement of dolphins increased the positive effects of craniosacral therapy.

The reason that dolphins are great helpers of craniosacral therapy is because of their sonar and vocalizations. The vibrations caused by such sounds mimic the craniosacral rhythm and cause a positive change in the body. Big cats are also used, as well, for the same reason. It's a reciprocal relationship, too – Kate said that many animals respond incredibly well to craniosacral therapy.

There are a few dolphin-assisted craniosacral therapy programs around if this is something that you're interested in.

Plus, you'd get the bonus of a tropical vacation, so it's a win-win! For example, Integrative Intentions runs a four-day intensive dolphin-assisted craniosacral therapy program in the Bahamas. During this program, you'll spend about 30 minutes per day with the dolphins; the rest of the day will be spent in craniosacral sessions with only human practitioners, either on land or in the water. Unfortunately, yet not unexpectedly, dolphin-assisted craniosacral therapy is quite pricey, even more so than regular craniosacral therapy, so keep your finances in mind if you're considering pursuing this method of healing.

Multi-Hands Craniosacral Therapy

Multi-hands craniosacral therapy is the same process as single-practitioner craniosacral therapy, but it involves more than one person. This method of craniosacral therapy is often used when an individual requires or desires intensive treatment. It's also common when the trauma is severe and complex; having multiple people involved in the therapy can expedite the healing process.

A Note About Craniosacral "Therapists"

There is no one certifying body for craniosacral therapy, and in fact, there is no professional licensure as a craniosacral therapist. Practitioners of craniosacral therapy need to have some other background that allows them to place their hands on you, such as nursing, massage therapy, or occupational therapy. For example, Kate's background is in physical therapy. Therefore, her title is a physical therapist who specializes in craniosacral therapy. Every craniosacral therapy practitioner brings their own individuality to the practice, so it's more important to find a practitioner that you resonate with on a personal level than to choose a practitioner based on their base licensure.

There are a number of schools that teach craniosacral therapy, though the largest and most structured is the Upledger Institute. Both the Upledger Institute and craniosacral therapy were founded by Dr. John Upledger from 1975 to 1985. The institute offers two basic and three advanced levels of craniosacral therapy training, as well as a variety of specialty courses and a certification program on the topic. There are practitioners all over the globe, and you can use this search tool if you're looking to find one in your area: www.iahp.com/pages/search/index.php.

Evidence Surrounding Craniosacral Therapy

Compared to other methods of therapy, such as EMDR or equine-assisted therapy, there is less research on the positive effects of craniosacral therapy, especially in regards to PTSD and those healing from trauma. The research can be categorized into two categories: studies that address trauma specifically and studies that address potential symptoms of trauma that arise from other conditions. The relevance of the former is obvious, but why is the latter important? Because of complex and childhood trauma (or ACEs), there are a wealth of symptoms and conditions that arise in adulthood that live under the name of a different diagnosis but can have their roots in trauma. Therefore, there's a potential that the conditions that craniosacral therapy has been proven to help could address your top layer of trauma symptoms: the conditions caused by your ACEs or past traumas. Even further, two of the studies that I'm about to describe show that craniosacral therapy is effective at helping any and all symptoms that the participants presented with. While it would be an inaccurate stretch to say that craniosacral therapy is a cure-all for everything, including all trauma symptoms, the research does lend itself to answering affirmatively the question of whether craniosacral therapy can help those healing from a trauma, especially if they're exhibiting somatic or mental health symptoms. Without further ado, here are a few studies on the effects of craniosacral therapy on a variety of conditions:

- Wetzler and colleagues in 2017 found that 10 sessions of craniosacral therapy were effective in decreasing pain and improving sleep length in veterans who suffered traumatic brain injuries.
- In 2017, Kratz, Kerr, and Porter showed that one to five weekly sessions of craniosacral therapy showed improvement in children and adolescents with autism spectrum disorder in their general behavior, cognitive function, communication, sensory reaction, social skills, and emotional stability. More specifically (and more relevant to trauma symptoms), it was reported that the recipients of craniosacral therapy were calmer and less anxious after sessions, showed increased eye contact and social communication, were more comfortable with physical contact, and showed decreased pain and

improved sleep.

- A study by Arnadottir and Sigurdardottir in 2013 concluded that craniosacral therapy was effective at decreasing scores on the HIT-6 test – a questionnaire that examines a migraine's effects on social and cognitive functioning and psychological distress – meaning that craniosacral therapy can help minimize the effects of migraines.

- Mataran-Penarrocha and colleagues and Castro-Sanchez and colleagues, both in 2011, found that two sessions of craniosacral therapy per week for 20-25 weeks showed decreased anxiety, depression, pain, and heart rate variability and increased sleep and quality of life in patients with fibromyalgia, and these effects were still present one year after the conclusion of the treatment.

- In 1999, Hanten et al. found that one ten-minute session of craniosacral therapy showed a significant decrease in pain from tension type headaches.

- A systematic review of seven studies on the effects of craniosacral therapy by Jakel and Hauenschild in 2012 found that the most commonly reported positive outcomes of craniosacral therapy were increased general well-being and quality of life and decreased pain, no matter what condition they presented with. Improved emotional state and sleep quality were close seconds in the list of common improvements.

- A qualitative study of clients' perspectives on craniosacral therapy completed by Brough et al. in 2015 showed similar outcomes as the Jakel and

Hauenschild review: improved presenting symptoms, no matter the cause of their symptoms.

As I previously described, there is also a collection of studies on the positive effects of craniosacral therapy for PTSD and trauma itself. The first study, conducted by Davis, Hanson, and Gilliam in 2016, concluded that two hour-long sessions of craniosacral therapy were effective in reducing anxiety related to PTSD. Two other studies, one by Perry, Perry, Boltuch, and Sisco and one by Upledger et al., examined the effects of intensive craniosacral therapy programs on veterans with PTSD. Both studies showed significant decreases in PTSD symptoms, anxiety, depression, and fatigue and increases in social function, sleep quality, and positive relationships with the therapists.

More convincingly, perhaps, are the anecdotes on the efficacy of craniosacral therapy. Dana, a woman who was raped and thrown off of a 75-foot cliff while serving in the Navy, received craniosacral therapy for her physical and emotional trauma. Aside from the incredible physical healing that has happened for Dana because of craniosacral therapy, she's had immense emotional healing, as well. "There were memories locked into my body that I actually had completely blocked and didn't remember until going through [my first craniosacral therapy] session," Dana described. "I pretty much relived the night of my injury in different phases and remembered things that I didn't even know happened. It wasn't fun, but it was really good. Emotionally, I'm more free. I can actually say this [story] without crying." Dana went on to describe how beginning craniosacral therapy was like digging through all of the muck of her trauma, clearing it out, and leaving a clean meadow in its wake. I, personally, am pretty impressed, as well, that the healing she described happened in just one session.

Another incredible story of the effects of craniosacral therapy is the story of a 56-year-old military veteran who was diagnosed with PTSD from a helicopter crash. He was suffering with depression, anxiety, and troubles connecting with others alongside his PTSD. He completed a five-day intensive craniosacral therapy program, and by day three, he was able to rid himself of "a 100lb backpack of" survivor's guilt by reframing the circumstance in his mind. At the end of the program, he was significantly more excited for his future and was optimistic about his ability to connect with significant people in his life.

The Upledger Institute runs a 20-hour intensive PTSD program, and the participants there have had some powerful testimonials of their own healing to share. Their expressed benefits include reframing the significance of trauma in their life, understanding that they're not alone, creating pathways for dealing with stress and triggers, releasing the trauma from their mind *and* body, and breaking down barriers to healthy relationships. If you'd like to learn more about the program and read the testimonials word-for-word, please visit www.upledger.com/ptsd.

Why did I write such a long explanation of the research and survivor anecdotes surrounding craniosacral therapy when I don't do the same for all the other methods of healing addressed in this book? I did it because I was immensely skeptical when I heard about this method of therapy, and I presume that you might be, as well. The science of cerebrospinal fluid levels and feeling energy trapped in the body with bare hands seemed "out-there" and, quite frankly, ridiculous. I actually struggled quite a bit with whether to include craniosacral therapy in this book because I want this to be an accurate guide and resource for you. My debate and uncertainty led me to do extensive research on the literature that's available on the topic. I decided that if there was enough convincing literature, I'd include it; if there wasn't, I'd scrap it. The literature I found combined with the anecdotes convinced me that it was a legitimate therapeutic method, and I figured that some of my readers – perhaps you – would need to see the literature to be convinced yourself. What was even more convincing to me, though, was my personal experience with craniosacral therapy.

My Experience with Craniosacral Therapy

Because of my skepticism, I wanted to experience craniosacral therapy for myself, so I met with Janet Crow of Twin Cities Craniosacral for a session of my own. Mind you, I didn't go in to work on trauma; I went in to work on my injured left shoulder and some lower back tension, but the effects were still incredibly noticeable. Janet worked on me for about an hour, and perhaps halfway through, I fell into a deep meditative state. Now, Janet told me beforehand that some people stay awake the whole time, some people fall into a semi-sleep state, and some people fall into a deep sleep, snoring and all. I fell into that middle group. My brain was running 100 miles an hour, as it usually does, during the first part of the session, and then I started to drift away. I was focusing less on noticing sensations in my body from a scientific perspective and thinking about how I was going to write this part of the book and started just kind of being. I felt her hands on me, but I didn't concentrate on them. I still had thoughts drifting through my brain, but I didn't obsess over or converse with them. I was just *being*, and all of a sudden, Janet was bringing me back to the present and telling me that we had five minutes left in session.

I noticed two significant benefits (beyond the relaxation) from just this one hour of craniosacral therapy. First of all, I had some pretty tight muscles in my neck from the shoulder injury and from recent workouts, and at the end of the session, that tension was pretty much gone. I found this particularly interesting, as craniosacral therapy is not massage. She did not massage the soreness out of my muscles; something else was at play there, and I have to believe that it was her work with my craniosacral rhythm. The second benefit requires a bit of an embarrassing admission. When I'm on my period, I don't get cramps or anything like that; I just get a very annoying lower back ache when I'm trying to sleep. It feels like my back really needs to pop but won't. Anyway, I explained this to Janet and asked her to work on my lower back because it was my time of the month. While my back wasn't sore during the session (so I didn't feel any immediate benefits), I slept like a baby that night with absolutely no lower back discomfort. Again, this wasn't massage or chiropractic work, so she didn't realign my pelvis or sacrum to relieve the tension. No, it was craniosacral therapy doing what it's supposed to. This was really incredible to me, as really nothing works long-term to alleviate the discomfort in my back when I'm on my period and trying to sleep. Icing it helps until the ice melts and my back warms back up. Trying to pop it works, but only if it pops, which it rarely does. This time, though, I have craniosacral therapy to thank for a night of peaceful and ache-free sleep.

An additional fact adds to my positive first impression of craniosacral therapy, and that is that I didn't go to Janet with any significant problems, emotional or physical. I had a little bit of tension here, and a little bit of discomfort there. Plus, she only worked on me for about an hour. I firmly believe, after my experience, that individuals with significant physical or emotional pain that went to craniosacral therapy for multiple sessions would see immense benefits. If you're skeptical, then take the word of a former skeptic who proved herself wrong: craniosacral therapy works. If you still don't believe me, I would highly suggest trying a session for yourself before completely disregarding it as a potential healing option.

Chapter 9:
Mindfulness and Meditation

ೞೞ

Meditation in trauma healing is something to approach with relative caution because its efficacy is variable depending on who you are and how you've reacted to your trauma. In order to understand this, it's important to understand the basic effects of childhood trauma. For someone who had a relatively safe childhood, they have a basic understanding that many situations are safe, and they feel comfortable being calm. For those who have had extensive childhood trauma, though, they've never had an example of a positive attachment, and they're more comfortable living in a hypervigilant state. "The more they relax, the more activated and scared and protective they become. For this person, the world is not safe, so to go into a meditative state is terrifying," Barbara explained.

In order to understand this better, imagine that you're in a room surrounded by people. One of them has a knife. One of them has a gun. One of them is smiling creepily in your direction. Now imagine being asked to close your eyes and relax in that room. Impossible, right? Who can protect you if you're in a meditative state? How can you see what's coming for you when your eyes are closed? That's how meditation can feel to someone who is more comfortable being hypervigilant or, in general, someone who strongly believes that the world is unsafe.

Even if you don't believe that the world is unsafe or suffer from dissociative episodes because of your trauma history, meditation and relaxation can be quite difficult because of controlling your breath. Tracey once had a client who was a former Navy SEAL. Part of learning to shoot is learning to control your breath, so when Tracey would ask him to practice breathing exercises, he would be brought right back to his time as a SEAL and to killing people. Luckily, relaxing and meditation are not required parts of healing or even of being mindful.

Instead of breath control or meditation being the goal, the goal is to gain a sense of control over the mind and the body. "The goal is to learn that they have power, that they don't have to follow where their brain goes," Tracey explained. "If you're able to relax as a result of this, great, that's a bonus, but that's not really why I'm trying to get you to [be mindful]. The reason I'm trying to get you to do this is to have some control over your mind because, a lot of times, people with trauma histories are a little bit out of control, impulsive, say things when they shouldn't be saying things, and do things when they need to stop and think before they do something. They can't do that because they don't have any control over their brains." This isn't calling you out or blaming you for the way that you act. It's not a fault of yours, but a side effect of your trauma that will heal as you do. If you find yourself frequently feeling out of control and craving a bit more discipline over your brain, then mindfulness or meditation would be a great addition to your healing journey.

As with many other therapies, the goal is to find something that works for you instead of working toward one, specific goal of relaxation and meditation. Meditation is a great way to achieve mindfulness, but if it doesn't work for you, then you need to find another way to be mindful – and it doesn't have to be something that's scary or makes you feel unsafe. "You can be mindfully washing dishes. You can be mindfully brushing your teeth. You can be mindfully walking," Tracey said. "You're actively doing something, and therefore, you are not relaxing." Regardless of whether you use meditation or another method to achieve mindfulness, the desired end result is the ability to bring your mind back to the same place, essentially on command.

That being said, meditation doesn't have to be an all or nothing approach. For example, some people cannot comfortably close their eyes and meditate, but they can achieve that same state of meditation and mindfulness if they can keep their eyes open and focused on an object or space in front of them. As I've said multiple times before, the gist of it is that if it works for you, it works for you. If you can meditate in a traditional manner and gain benefit and mindfulness from it, all the more power to you. If you can achieve a meditative and relaxed state but need some modifications, then you can make that work. If you can't meditate at all, then there are other ways to achieve mindfulness. Remember, the goal here isn't to sit cross-legged and say "om" for an hour; it's to learn to control your brain so you can choose to respond, as opposed to react, when you're triggered.

Another common issue with meditation is that it's *hard.* If you've ever tried to calm your brain down and relax for a period of time, you'll believe me when I say this. I'll tell the full story at the beginning of the yoga chapter, but when I tried to meditate for an hour the first time, it took 30 minutes of my brain going every which way and of me yelling at it to calm down for me to actually be able to breathe and relax. Many people experience this same struggle the first time they try meditation, believe they're not good at it or that it doesn't work for them, and give up on the whole process. If you're finding this happens with you, remember that Rome wasn't built in a day. In other words, everything takes practice to master – including meditation.

I played soccer for close to fourteen years and basketball for almost nine, so it goes without saying that I had really strong legs. Soccer thunder thighs were totally a thing for me. When I started training for the military, the biggest challenge I faced was swimming. I thought I'd be relatively decent at it; after all, I was in shape and I knew how to swim, even if I'd never lap swam before. My first time in the pool, I couldn't make it one length – 25 meters! – without my quads cramping up, and I couldn't make it a full lap without being incredibly out of breath and needing a break. I vividly remember one of the lifeguards chatting to me one day and asking how far I was swimming that day. I meekly said that I had 600m to swim, and he laughed and told me to have fun on my easy day. I turned my butt straight around back to the locker room, sat down in a shower stall, and cried. That was not the first or only time I cried on my swimming journey. I doubted whether I could ever learn to swim and berated myself for not being able to swim better more times than I'd like to count. I stuck with it, though, because my goal of being a pararescueman was more important to me than my pride or the opinion of one lifeguard. Now, I can swim for miles, and the water is the place where I can let go of all the everyday stresses and relax for a little while.

While my swimming story has nothing to do with meditation, it has to do exactly with what a lot of people think when they start meditation. I thought swimming would be relatively easy for me; many people think that meditation will be simple. I thought about quitting and giving up swimming because I couldn't do it; many people say that they can't meditate and give up on it as a healing mechanism. I stuck with swimming and learned to love it; the people who stick with meditation learn that it's a skill and that they can get better at it in order to reap its benefits. If you're struggling with meditation and think about giving up, think of me, running back to the locker room and crying in a completely dry swimsuit after the lifeguard told me that my workout (that I didn't end up doing that day) was equivalent to a recovery day. If I can conquer the water, you can conquer meditation.

Beyond the mental struggles of meditation, the process of learning to meditate is actually akin to training your muscles. To stick with my swimming story, I had to be able to swim 500m to enter the training pipeline and be able to fin 3000m to complete it. Each of those requirements had time limits on them, as well, limits that seemed impossible to meet when I started swimming – the 500m swim time limit was a little over 10 minutes, and the first 500m that I swam (mind you, with excessive breaks every lap) was 13:30. I worked at it, though, every single day. I was swimming four or five days a week, starting with reps of 50m and building up the distance the fitter I got. It wasn't long before I could swim 500m in a row, and it wasn't long after that that I could hit the time requirement needed for the pararescue pipeline. The day that I made that time was probably one of the proudest days of my life. It took work, it took consistency, and it took dedication, and your journey to being able to meditate successfully requires the same things. It might take two weeks or it might take six months, but you have to train your brain like a muscle learning a new task in order to be able to meditate if you've never done so before.

A great way to start a meditation practice is to start with simply five minutes. Work on being conscious, present, and mindful for five minutes, and even if you feel your brain jumping all over the place, your goal is to bring it back every time. You can practice this through traditional meditation or through an activity like washing the dishes. If you're meditating in a traditional manner, then focus on bringing your mind back to your breath. If you're meditating while washing dishes, for example, then bring yourself back to the action of washing dishes when your mind starts to wander. As you start to gain better control of your mind, you'll be able to meditate for longer and longer sessions. Now, that's not to say that the ultimate meditation goal is to be able to sit in the mountains for a week in a Zen state and meditate every minute of your life. Again, the goal of meditation is to learn to control your mind better so that you can respond instead of react in stressful or triggering situations, so a good time goal for meditation is twenty minutes per day.

Various Types of Meditation

After I spent all this time talking about how meditation (as opposed to mindfulness) can be anywhere from dangerous to ineffective for survivors of trauma, you're probably expecting me to conclude this chapter by saying to stay away from meditation. Luckily, that's not the case. If you're able to meditate safely – and that's the key phrase here – then it can be a very helpful tool in learning mindfulness and regaining control of your mind's reactions. There are various types of meditation that can be helpful for trauma survivors, but make sure to consult your therapist or medical provider before starting these processes. Meditation may seem like something simple and harmless, but delving into the depths of your mind and your trauma without proper and professional guidance can set you back multiple steps in your healing journey.

Loving-Kindness Meditation

Self-compassion is often lacking in someone that has experienced a trauma. It's not uncommon for the individual to turn the negative feelings they have about their traumatic experience to themselves, directing that hatred and anger inside. This, obviously, is not helpful in the healing process, and the loving-kindness meditation method focuses on increasing levels of self-compassion. When you look back at the traumatic experience that you've been through, fear is commonly the first emotion that comes into your being, and loving-kindness meditation works to transition that fear to love and acceptance of yourself and others.

Loving-kindness meditation is based on the mental concentration of positive thoughts to various people in your life. The practice starts with an easy one: thinking of someone you hold a positive opinion of and mentally blessing them. The four most common blessings are "may you be safe", "may you be happy", "may you be healthy", and "may your life unfold with ease". After you bestow those blessings on someone that you think positively of, loving-kindness meditation moves to thinking of someone who you think neither positively nor negatively of, yourself, and finally someone who you think negatively of, then repeating the process with each of those individuals.

A pilot study by Kearney et al. in 2013 showed immense benefits from a relatively simple schedule of loving-kindness meditation: 45 minutes, once per week, for nine weeks. Each week, according to the model studied by Kearney et al., should focus on a different individual or set of individuals, including:

- Someone you think positively of
- Yourself
- A close friend, human or otherwise
- Yourself and someone you think positively of
- Someone you think neither positively nor negatively of
- Someone who has caused you harm (perhaps the person responsible for your trauma)

After the end of a simple course of nine weeks of loving-kindness meditation, the individuals who participated in the study showed significantly increased feelings of self-compassion and decreased negative symptoms related to their trauma, and these benefits lasted for months after they finished the nine weeks of loving-kindness meditation.

Transcendental Meditation

Transcendental meditation is a decades-old meditation practice that's quite popular with many populations because of its ease of practice. There's no visualization, no concentration on thoughts, and no requirements of emptying the mind. The focus is on the repetition of a sound without meaning – some sort of mantra – that brings your brain to a quieter level of thought, moves you into a state of restful awareness, and allows you transcend yourself and connect with your consciousness. If that sounds a little scary or a little vague, don't worry. Transcendental meditation is practiced under the guidance of a certified instructor, usually for two twenty-minute sessions daily for four days.

The benefits of transcendental meditation have been studied extensively, and they are quite incredible, as well. The major categories of benefits fall into decreased stress and anxiety, improved brain function, and improved cardiovascular health, but there are many benefits more specific to trauma and PTSD. Studies by Nidich et al. in both 2016 and 2017 found that transcendental meditation programs showed significant decreases in overall trauma symptoms, anxiety, depression, intrusive thoughts, dissociation, hyperarousal, sleep disturbances, and stress in traumatized inmates, and studies by Barnes, Rigg, and Williams and by Rosenthal, Grosswald, Ross, and Rosenthal in 2013 and 2011 respectively showed that transcendental meditation helped veterans with PTSD become calmer, more patient, more positive, more energetic, more alert, less irritable, and less anxious. Furthermore, many of the participants in these studies reported improved sleep, and all of them showed significant decreases in overall trauma symptoms. Perhaps most interestingly, everyone who participated in transcendental meditation enjoyed the practice and were still seeing the positive results eight to twelve weeks after they finished their course of meditation, according to the two PTSD studies and an additional study by Rees et al. in 2014.

If you don't trust the research, trust the over six million people who have participated in and benefitted from transcendental meditation. If you've spoken with your therapist and/or feel like transcendental meditation would be a good fit for you and your healing journey, then visit www.tm.org and click the orange button in the top right corner to find a certified teacher in your area.

Breathing-Based Meditation

When you're scared or remembering a scary event, what happens? Among other things, your breathing rate picks up, and that creates and holds on to tension throughout your body. Therefore, it makes sense that a controlled breathing exercise would help regulate your emotions regarding a past traumatic incident. The benefits of breathing-based meditation are well-studied and are quite impressive, as well, so it makes for a powerful healing method. That being said, know yourself, just as Tracey's ex-SEAL knew himself. If controlling your breathing leads to triggers of traumatic memories, then consider another meditation practice or a mindfulness-based approach.

Breathing-based meditation is, as you probably guessed, all about regulating your breathing and allowing that to calm and center you. These intentional breaths generally fall into one of four categories (for reference, the standard adult breathing rate is 12 to 20 breaths per minute):

- Victorious Breath: breathing at a rate of two to four breaths per minute
- Bellows Breath: breathing at a rate of 30 breaths per minute
- Om Chants: repeating the "om" sound, stretching out each syllable
- Proper Vision by Purifying Action: rhythmic and cycled breaths at slow, medium, and fast paces

These four breaths are particularly common in Sudarshan Kriya yoga, one form of breathing-based meditation. It is recommended that you practice breathing-based meditation daily, even if that means you only get a few cycles of intentional breath in. It shouldn't be stressful to add it to your day, so you don't have to commit to an hour a day of meditation if that's not something that would fit easily in your schedule. That being said, it's also not something that should be an afterthought; a key point of meditation is intention.

Breathing-based meditation, as already touched on, can produce benefits such as reduced post-traumatic stress symptoms, improved mood, decreased anxiety, and lasting reduced respiration rate, and a study by Seppala et al. in 2014 showed that these benefits can still exist even a year after a concentrated week of breathing-based meditation. Even more interestingly, out of their participants who continued to practice breathing-based meditation, there was no difference in reported mood or symptoms between those who practiced once per month and those who practiced daily. In other words, their study showed that a hefty dose of breathing-based meditation followed by occasional reinforcement produced significant and long-lasting results. Beyond benefits specifically related to PTSD and trauma, breathing-based meditation has been shown to increase optimism, quality of life, emotional regulation, and immune function and decrease depression, impulsive behavior, and substance use in a wide variety of populations, from college students to cancer patients.

My Personal Choice for Meditation

When I started my meditation journey, I really struggled with calming my mind down, as I explained before. My mind runs at a million miles an hour every single minute of the day, constantly bouncing from idea to idea and from to-do item to a concept for the future. I'm a professional dreamer and a master list maker, and my brain acts accordingly. I practiced, though, just as I did with swimming, and now I have a simple five-minute meditative process that I go through almost every day. I personally like the five-minute timespan because it's something that I can easily commit to, even when my days are busy, and because I can do that pretty much anywhere, whether that's right before bed or in between classes in a quiet room on campus.

I start my meditation practice by getting into a position I'm comfortable in; for me, that means lying down on my back. Sitting up and focusing on breath and posture might work really well for some people, but all that does for me is force me to focus on the tension in my back when all I'm trying to do is relax. I also love using essential oils while meditating. I have a blend of wintergreen, lavandin, eucalyptus, coriander, olibanum, rosemary, chamomile, peppermint, basil and origanum that I love – it sounds like a lot, but it comes in a pre-made blend. I don't put it on my body; rather, I open the bottle and sit it next to me while I meditate. If I have a candle, I'll definitely darken the room and light that, too.

After I set up my meditation space and find a comfortable position, I start at the top of my body and focus on systematically relaxing every muscle that I have – and I mean *every muscle*. Usually, I start with my forehead and my eyes and make sure that I'm not clenching them shut or forcing them open. Then I move down to my mouth – is that being held in a certain position or is it allowed to relax as it wants to? After that comes my neck and shoulders. I hold tension and stress in my shoulders, so focusing on relaxing them down towards my toes is a key point for me. Then, like I said, it's muscle by muscle, making sure that no muscle is forcing my body to stay in a certain position and allowing each and every part of my body to relax into the floor or bed and release whatever stress it's been carrying.

It's after this whole process that I start to focus on my breath and calm my mind down. I don't really have a scientific process for this; it's more about bringing my mind back to my breath when it wanders and continually checking in with my body to make sure that I don't start clenching my muscles again. After my five-minute meditation sessions, I feel much calmer and clearer about my goals for the day, and I feel as if there's a blanket of peace that covers me. While there's no empirical backing to my meditation practice or my experiences with it, it helps me nearly every day and it'd be a great place to start if your therapist has tasked you with some at-home meditation practice.

Benefits of Meditation and Mindfulness

As you can see, there are a few choices for meditation options, all with their own set of benefits and practices. Rest assured, though, that if you decide to pursue an alternative method of mindfulness or meditation, you'll still receive some amazing benefits. It's more than just feeling better or feeling calmer, too; meditation actually enacts a relaxation response and changes the way your brain behaves. These changes result in lowered respiration rates, heart rates, and blood pressure and positive changes in brain regions associated with attention, concentration, interoception, sensory processing, inhibition, motivation, and memories of emotions.

Specifically for individuals who have experienced trauma, meditation can be incredibly beneficial because of the self-determination theory proposed by Deci and Ryan in 1980. This theory states that self-awareness is critical in making decisions that align with your goals, values, and beliefs, decisions that many trauma survivors could not make because of their traumatic situation and the events surrounding it. When you're more mindful of your present life, you're more likely to make decisions that align with your current needs and goals, as opposed to the potentially survival-based decisions you were making in the past. This awareness of the present situation helps you differentiate between what's the reality of your past trauma and what's the present reality, as well. Finally, meditation gives trauma survivors a piece of their power back that they likely lost during the traumatic event. Meditation is built on the concept that each individual has the internal strength to create resources and coping mechanisms for navigating life; in other words, meditation acknowledges that you are strong, powerful, and completely capable of running your own life. This is a very powerful revelation for many trauma survivors.

Mindfulness, too, has some very positive benefits beyond learning to control your mind and its knee-jerk reactions better. Mindfulness practices, like meditation, have been shown to decrease anxiety, depression, stress, substance use, and chronic pain and improve emotional regulation and quality of life. Furthermore, mindfulness brings with it a healthy dose of self-awareness, which can help bring the attention into the present, differentiate that from the past, and build a skillset of self-regulation. Finally, mindfulness has been shown to decrease PTSD symptoms, specifically that of avoidance.

How to Integrate Mindfulness and Meditation into Your Trauma Therapy Program

The broad answer to this is somewhat simple: express your interest in including mindfulness and/or meditation in your trauma therapy program and work with your therapist to create a plan to make that happen. It might start with meditation in the office, like Tracey does, and work up to meditation and mindfulness practices as homework or the homework might start right away, but you and your therapist can figure out what's going to be best for you. Regardless, about half of mental health professionals will both incorporate meditation or mindfulness into your therapy program and help you create mindfulness practices to use in your daily life, so it's not likely to be a struggle for you to add mindfulness or meditation to your therapy program.

It's also important to note that there is no standard training protocol for meditation and mindfulness use like there is for many other therapy methods. In fact, almost 20% of mindfulness and meditation teachers received no formal training, and the vast majority of people who do receive training receive it from another mental health professional. This is both somewhat helpful and somewhat worrisome. The good news is that you won't be limited in therapist choice based on who has some meditation or mindfulness certification, but the bad news is that there's no certifying body that ensures that they're adequately educated to help you with meditation and mindfulness practices. Don't worry, though – about 88% of people who teach mindfulness and meditation to their clients practice it in their own lives, so they're not totally winging it; they're working with you from a history of both personal experience and the experiences of other clients.

Chapter 10:
Dance–Movement
Therapy

CRBO

D ance-movement therapy is, out of the various therapeutic modalities discussed in this book, the one that pulls most heavily on the somatic aspect of trauma – the part that's stored in the body. Don't worry, though; it's not traditional dance, so you won't be expected to tango across the room to heal from trauma. Dance-movement therapy came out of the American modern dance movement that started in the '40s when people realized that they were getting some personal development and self-discovery out of dancing. Therefore, the name has its base in dance, but the actual practice of therapy can look like a lot of different things, including but not limited to dance-like movements.

Barbara Nordstrom-Loeb, the dance-movement therapist I've previously spoken of and quoted, describes the practice as "the broadest umbrella in-depth way of working the body-mind. It's a creative arts therapy in its approach, so it works psychologically, but it really works with mind-body, body-mind." Though the "mind-body connection" might seem a little woo-woo, it's simply another way of describing the relationship between the mind and body and a way of approaching healing through both the mind *and* body. This is critical in trauma healing and is one of the major pitfalls of cognitive behavioral therapy and traditional talk therapy for trauma survivors.

One huge advantage of dance-movement therapy is its ability to work around words. Words can be problematic in a variety of situations. First of all, because trauma is such a full-body experience, putting all of your reactions to your traumatic event into words can be difficult, if not impossible. Secondly, the deep effects of trauma can make you not want to speak or not be able to speak, which renders all forms of talk therapy nearly impossible for you. Thirdly, there are vast cultural differences in reactions to trauma that make taking the words at face-value difficult. For example, some cultures don't express emotions as freely as other cultures, so individuals of that culture who experience trauma will exhibit more somatic symptoms. In other words, instead of saying that they're feeling angry or in pain emotionally, they would say that they feel a fire burning inside of them. Luckily, everyone has a body and every body speaks, so dance-movement therapy can be an outlet for individuals for whom words don't suffice or for those whose cultural views of trauma have them expressing their feelings in a different manner.

In fact, in many dance-movement therapy practices, the bodily sensations and the words used to describe the emotions are not distinguished between. "Emotion is the name of the body experience," Barbara explained. "Infants don't think, 'Oh, I'm happy!'; they have a physical experience in their body and they express it." Trauma expression can be a similar experience, especially because it's such a base reaction. Furthermore, some people use the verbal expression to avoid the physical sensation, whereas other people describe the bodily sensation because it's easier or more comfortable, perhaps because of cultural or gender norms. In dance-movement therapy, it's not useful to spend time differentiating between the two, as they're pretty much the same thing. The benefit to understanding the differences, though, is that the therapist can then see how the person is relating to their trauma.

Goals of Dance-Movement Therapy

Regaining Control

Many people who have experienced a trauma feel out of control, unsafe, or weak, so a goal of dance-movement therapy is to allow you to feel strong and in-control again. "We might do some stamping. Sometimes I might have them feel a core of energy, like they're rooted as a tree," Barbara described when asked what happens during a dance-movement therapy session. If it's too unsafe and uncomfortable for you to come back into your body because of the trauma that lives in it, Barbara also described that she might ask you to envision being your favorite superhero and feel what it feels like to be them.

Many of the movements in dance-movement therapy, such as envisioning yourself rooted as a tree or as your favorite superhero, are aimed at helping you connect with your core and your sense of self. When you connect with your core through movements like these, you start to connect with parts of your body that respond to emotions and, in turn, crystalize that connection with the self. "Becoming aware of our core or our inner experiences helps us to authentically develop a deeper sense of who we are, as well as a sense of resilience and agency," Barbara explained when asked about what "feeling a core of energy" was. "Finding ways to engage the core is an important goal for many since it helps us feel authentic and supports truthful expression in the world." This connection ultimately helps you feel more empowered, connected to the world, and in control.

This goal can also be accomplished by literally allowing you to have more control over the situation. "I'll say, 'Where do you want me to sit? I can sit further away or, if you want, I can face away from you,'" Barbara explained. She even offers some clients the choice to ask her to close her eyes so that they don't feel like she's judging them or placing any expectations on them. This shifts the power from the person in authority – the therapist – to the person receiving the therapy. "For them to feel safe, what they need is to feel like they're in control, that they have power," Barbara added. Having control over this one therapy session can set the groundwork for reestablishing control in daily life.

Completing the Cycle

Another goal of dance-movement therapy is allowing for the completion of the cycle of emotions and energy that's started during a traumatic event. In many traumatic events, there's an action that you want to take or an emotion that you want to express but cannot, either because you physically can't or because you know it would make the situation worse. For example, a child living in an abusive household might want to lash out and cry, but they know that it would only make their night a lot more painful. Therefore, they don't, and that cycle of energy, emotion, and expression is halted, unable to be completed.

When you're able to complete that action that you wanted to do during your trauma, it's common for a large part of your trauma to be released from you. "All of the hormones and chemistry that our brain activates so that we can defend ourselves – if it's not used up, it sort of gets held and stored in the body," Barbara explained. Dance-movement therapy is a safe way for the body to complete that cycle – the keyword being safe. "If it just comes out at the intensity [of the trauma], it feels out of control and that can be more terrifying. It feels good in the moment, but it can become very overwhelming." If that's the case – if that release becomes overwhelming and frightening – there's a very good chance that you won't pursue that method of healing again, therefore never allowing your body to complete the cycle and release that bomb of emotions.

This is why it's incredibly critical to have a trained mental health professional on your team, as I talked about in the introduction to the various therapeutic methods. They are able to create a safe environment for you to let out those emotions in a controlled manner and they're able to recognize when you're getting out of control and rein you back in. Even if you're in a controlled environment with a trained therapist, you're likely not going to start with a dramatic release. It's more important for both you and the therapist to understand your mental "escape routes" and how you come back to a safe space before delving into the releasing of it.

When that trauma does start to release, though, it usually does so in a layered process, and it often doesn't start with the rehashing of your traumatic event. "What sometimes happens is, as something gets moved and released, then the story will come out," Barbara explained. She went on to tell the story of a client who was adopted from Asia into a "sketchy family" – her words. This client just wanted to push, so Barbara provided a pillow for her to push against. When she was able to successfully push the pillow away from her, she was able to recognize a piece of her trauma that was released and her cycle was completed: her brother raped her, and all she wanted to do in that instant was push her brother away.

It's important to note that one instance of releasing or one cycle completed doesn't mean that your whole trauma journey is complete. Trauma, especially if it happened multiple times or over a long period of time, has many layers, and as one layer is released, another one is exposed and needs healing. There's nothing wrong with you for needing to do this, and you're not failing in your healing journey if this is the case. Actually, it's the opposite – you're succeeding, and it's time to succeed again.

Coming Back into Your Body

A third goal of dance-movement therapy is called pendulation, which is the process of going into your traumatic event in your mind and then returning to the present and to your body. As you look back toward your trauma and then return to a grounded, safe state in your adult self, you gain practice doing that in the real world, which can be essential in reshaping your reactions and managing triggers or flashbacks. "It's really about how I can support them going back into the memory," Barbara explained. "That's the challenge: how to do it in a way that feels manageable and controllable."

One way that dance-movement therapists can help create that safe space is to ask questions. For example, Barbara explained that when someone was revisiting the memory of their trauma and found a particularly scary individual, for example, she would ask them if they could, while in session, move far enough away from their visualization of that individual so that the individual they're recalling couldn't hurt them. As the client physically moved away from their trauma, they created a metaphor that could be applied to moving away from their trauma in real life. This is very similar to the EAGALA model of equine-assisted therapy, as you'll learn later in the book.

What Happens During Dance-Movement Therapy

Though we've discussed this a little bit so far, I wanted to go into more detail about what happens during a session of dance-movement therapy. Barbara explained that the first thing she'd do is try to get an understanding of what you know about your trauma, what methods of healing you've pursued so far, and how it's impacting your life. "When I start with clients, I also want to get a sense of what their relationship is with their body," Barbara added. To do this, she would start by asking you what, if anything, you're noticing in your body. Don't try to trick her out of answering this question by saying that "it feels fine", either. If you give your therapist an answer like that, she'll turn it back around on you: "Oh, okay, well which area feels more fine than others?" This goes as a general rule of thumb for all therapeutic methods, but if you're going to go to therapy, *go to therapy*. There's no benefit to half-assing it or giving fake answers; you're there to heal, and heal you will, no matter how hard, scary, or emotional it may be.

This part of the therapy is all about building trust between you and the therapist. Even if you recognize something in your body and relate that to your traumatic event, there's a good chance that the therapist will acknowledge that, remember it, and move on to asking about a body part that feels the opposite of that area that feels like trauma. Delving too deep too quickly can be harmful, but don't dismiss the recognition that an area of your body feels a certain way *because* of trauma. Your therapist will make note of it, and later down the therapeutic road, movement will take place that can help release that trauma. Just don't rush there.

Anyway, after the therapist finds out what happens and how you feel when you bring your bodily sensations into your conscious awareness, she'll start to delve into the sensory sensations. For example, if you say that your shoulders feel tight because you were shoveling snow, the next level would be to explore how tight it feels, whether it feels equally tight on both sides, whether it feels hot or cold, and things like that. At this point (and if you're not already doing so), movement will start to come into the session with the golden question: "If your shoulder could move, how would it want to move?" The key here is to allow your body to move how it wants to, instead of having the brain come in and resist the movement or try to move it to a more "normal" place. To be clear, dance-movement therapy is not physical therapy or massage. The goal is not to work out sore muscles or realign joints or anything like that. Oftentimes, physical sensations are the top, top layer of trauma, and dance-movement therapy starts there and uses that sensation as a way to delve down, layer by layer, into and through your trauma.

Beyond you moving your body in the way that it wants to go, there are a few other powers at play that help the therapist guide the session. First is that of somatic countertransference, which is a long term that basically means that the therapist feels what you're feeling in their body. This occurs through a combination of the therapist's gut feeling and their ability to pick up on changes in your breathing and bodily tension. The second is kinesthetic empathy, which is the phenomenon of feeling like you're experiencing movements in your own body that you're actually only watching. The combination of kinesthetic empathy and somatic countertransference allows the therapist to feel, in a way, what you're feeling, and when he or she is able to differentiate between what you're feeling and what he or she is actually feeling in her own body, she can use those findings as a guide for progression in your therapy. "I will use what I'm sensing in my own body to get suggestions, to guide the things I'm getting curious about," Barbara explained. The third power at play is the consistent neurophysiological piece of trauma. As Barbara said and I wrote above, that piece is pretty consistent across individuals and across cultures, and with experience, a good dance-movement therapist will understand the neurophysiology of trauma and how to conduct therapy based on that framework.

After that, it's time for you to take the lead again. The therapist trusts your body and trusts that it knows the movements it needs, so this is your time to move in a way that feels right to you while the therapist takes the backseat. "Whenever I get ahead of myself and think I know what their body wants, usually the body wants something else," Barbara said while laughing. "It kind of puts you back in your place!" At this point, it's all about what comes up in your body. Sometimes, the therapist might give shape and form to what comes up, but the body knows what's right, and as Barbara said – guidance or forcefulness can get in the way. Rather, the therapist's goal is to find safe methods for it to move so you can complete your cycle of that movement. Appropriately expressed anger? Great! It helps you feel your own power. A bit of role playing of positive and inspirational characters? Go for it. Whatever your body needs and whatever way your body wants to move, allow it to do so with openness and graciousness.

A quick note about that anger, though. When I talk about completing the cycle of energy generated during traumatic events, it can seem like dance-movement therapy is all about screaming and jumping and doing all sorts of crazy things. It's not always like that, and releasing the anger surrounding your trauma through methods like that isn't always the best (there are actually links between expressed hostility and heart disease!). Some healthy methods of releasing anger include running in a secluded area or diving underwater and SCREAMING out your anger or writing your feelings down then shredding the paper with a knife. Creative methods are always appreciated, and as long as you're controlled (read: not dissociating) and it's helpful to your healing journey and overall wellbeing, you've got an official stamp of approval to continue with it.

Benefits of Dance-Movement Therapy

It helps you release your trauma through movement and completing cycles – duh, right? Well, yes, but there's more to it. Dance-movement therapy has some very specific benefits and some very inspirational case studies to go along with it. Overall, dance-movement therapy accomplishes four goals within trauma survivors: making the connection between mind and body, increasing mobility and range of motion, creating a healthy physical relationship with yourself and others, and creating a new relationship with movement. These goals can be accomplished through a variety of methods, including metaphors, props, and the interactions between the survivor and the therapist, and the methods used will vary depending on the therapist you see and how you consciously or subconsciously lead the session.

In addition, when considering the impact of ACEs on adult health, it's common for people to have an improved relationship with their physiological health conditions because they understand them better. For example, instead of hating your body for your fibromyalgia and dreading the times it flares up, you can use it as a signal and learn to correlate it with events in your life. You might recognize that it flares up around times of extended social interaction, and from that, you can learn to push yourself a little less hard or get a little bit more support in your life. It's not that dance-movement therapy will heal every physiological problem that results from an ACE, but it can help you reshape your perception of and relationship with your body and its health issues.

Another important benefit of dance-movement therapy is learning that power does not have to be violent. Barbara told me a story of a client of hers who was absolutely terrified of his anger because he had grown up in a volatile and unsafe household. For him, punching pillows and ripping things allowed him to differentiate between the valuable and useless aspects of power. It allowed him to show up with his power and learn that there's nothing intrinsically wrong with being powerful and that power doesn't always equate to violence. For survivors of violent events, whether that's assault, rape, or something else entirely, power can often equate to violence, but partaking in dance-movement therapy, learning about correctly applied power, and establishing personal power can help correct that belief set and remove that fear of power.

Dance-movement therapy, though not commonly

conducted in this manner, can be a group or family activity designed to improve relationships between individuals, as shown by a case study by Devereaux in 2008. A family had been dramatically affected by domestic abuse. The children frequently had violent and emotional outbursts, which triggered the mom's memories of her husband's abuse, causing her to become fearful of her children. The family completed a variety of synchronized and unified movements under the care of the dance-movement therapist; for example, the therapist had the family connect hands, and she slowly wound them into a knot – a family knot – and instructed them to "untie the family knot". This simulated working through the struggles that they were experiencing as a unit, without fear or violent outbursts. The family also worked on exercises that helped them develop boundaries and personal space and recognize the mother as the leader of the family. After a few months of weekly therapy, the family's verbal communication improved, their anxiety decreased, the mother's leadership increased, and family fun and playfulness were reintroduced into their lives. It was because of the movements that served as metaphors in the family's life (the family knot, for example) that the family translated skills from therapy to reality and learned how to interact with one another again in a healthy manner.

Another incredible case study that shows the vast benefits of dance-movement therapy was written by Gray in 2001. It tells the story of a woman who was kidnapped, raped, beaten, and starved for a month after witnessing her brother being killed in front of her and after being physically ripped away from her children. Over the course of months of dance-movement therapy, this woman went from being a shell of herself – constant worry for her children, an inability to make eye contact, dissociation from her body, and withdrawn posture – to wanting to live, understanding that her emotions and physical sensations came from within her body, and inviting her therapist to share in a cultural dance from her past. In addition, her gait and posture improved, she was comfortable making eye contact, she was sleeping better, she felt safe in her body again, and she was comfortable interacting sexually with her husband. I definitely shed a tear when reading this full case study, as the amount of trauma that this woman overcame is absolutely incredible. It's in large part thanks to dance-movement therapy.

As you can tell with this woman's story, dance-movement therapy can be incredibly beneficial for individuals who have experienced physical violence, including sexual assault and sexual abuse. Through those types of violence, personal boundaries are destroyed and touch is turned into a monster. Dance-movement therapy provides an opportunity for safe, controllable touch and movement, which in turn gives the survivor a chance to reprogram their mind's perspective of physical contact and intimacy. More specifically, dance-movement therapy offers this opportunity through accomplishing an additional four goals: bodily awareness and acceptance, personal and interpersonal intimacy, increased ability to self-regulate and self-soothe, and an exploration of emotional states. These goals fall under the umbrella of recognizing the body as an ally in the healing process, which, when accomplished, results in an incredibly improved relationship with one's own body, something that can definitely suffer after a sexual assault.

A final benefit that's most useful for individuals who tend to dissociate is that the time it takes to return to a non-dissociative state can be greatly reduced. Dance-movement therapy won't necessarily remove all dissociative episodes, but it can greatly improve your management of and recovery from those episodes. "The goal [for these individuals] then becomes: 'Let's work on recognizing when it's happening and strategies for minimizing [time spent] being dissociated'," Barbara explained. Clients will start with taking two weeks to return to themselves from a dissociative episode, and with more dance-movement therapy, that timeline can be shortened to a week, then a couple of days, and then a handful of hours.

How are all these benefits possible, and why are they so commonly achieved in dance-movement therapy? Well, it has to do with the goals of the movement – rather, that there are no goals. Dance-movement therapy is a form of non-goal-oriented movement, meaning that there's no specific form for or objective of the movement. Traditional choreographed dance, for example, has a goal: complete the choreography. Dance-movement therapy is more about moving in a way that feels right for you and helps complete the cycle of your trauma. A study by Wiedenhofer, Hofinger, Wagner, and Kock in 2016 found that the non-goal-oriented nature of dance-movement therapy results in benefits that goal-oriented movement does not: decreased stress, improved well-being, and improved body self-efficacy. What does this mean for you, as a potential dance-movement therapy client? Don't go in with expectations for directions on how to move. Receiving

those and having goals for your movement can actually minimize the benefits you receive from dance-movement therapy,
so simply listen to your body and follow its lead.

My Experience with Dance-Movement Therapy

After I met Barbara for a dance-movement therapy session of my own, the two words that I'd use to describe dance-
movement therapy were uncomfortable and counterintuitive
(Barbara, I saw you wince when I said those words, but don't
you worry – I have nothing but good things to say about you
and the therapy). I really went into the session not knowing
what to expect. The vision that I had in my mind of dance-
movement therapy was a mood-lit dance studio and people
making large and dramatic movements across the room, but
that couldn't be further from the truth. Barbara and I sat on a
couch and just started talking. She blended the session between an actual therapy session and talking about what she
would do if I was actually her client. She asked me what I noticed in my body, and after pointing out that my shoulder was
a bit sore, it really started to get interesting.

This is where the counterintuitive part comes in. The
medical professional and the athlete in me started talking
about how I swam a lot the day before, so my shoulder was
sore, and it felt like I needed to roll or massage it out. Even
sitting there telling her about how it felt, I was massaging the
tightness out of my shoulder with my other hand. Barbara,
though, encouraged me to follow my shoulder's lead and do
what it was pulling to do, which was pull up toward my neck,

and see what came of it. It seemed to me like I was only encouraging the problem, but I went along with what she instructed me to do. As I slowly allowed my shoulder to creep up toward my neck, I noticed that my arms, which were lying in my lap, wanted to curl up, as well. I allowed them to, and as I followed the movement my body wanted to make, I ended up with my arms crossed over my neck and my fingers gripping at the collar of my shirt. This is where it got uncomfortable. For me, the position that I ended up in was very protective, weak, and almost cowering, and I felt vulnerable being that way in front of someone else.

It's important to know that my session with Barbara went way further than a traditional first session with a client would, primarily because the beginning sessions are all about creating a therapeutic relationship between the client and the therapist. If Barbara and I were working together – meaning she was my therapist and I was her client – that therapeutic relationship would have progressed over many sessions until I was much more comfortable forming that position with her. Therefore, my experience with dance-movement therapy is essentially multiple sessions condensed into one, so don't expect to go as far or feel as uncomfortable when you attend dance-movement therapy.

That being said, I still had an incredible experience with just this one session. Perhaps this is just my brain, but I immediately recognized what that position symbolized for me, as it's the same position that my body wants to take when I'm faced with physical or intimate contact with someone. Barbara and I spent some time discussing how my "therapy" would progress if I was an actual client, and she told me that we would explore the spectrums of strength and weakness and of being open and closed. In short, it's good to be open with people sometimes, but it's also good to be closed and protective of the vulnerable and deep parts of yourself. It's not a black-and-white weakness to be in a protective position.

This got me thinking about martial arts, as I am a jiu-jitsu practitioner and women's self-defense instructor. The final piece that we teach in women's self-defense seminars is about defense against rape scenarios where you are on your back and someone is between your legs. In jiu-jitsu, that position is actually called "guard". The women are always very uncomfortable when we start training that position, and I distinctly remember being uncomfortable myself when I started learning it. After all, who wants some stranger in between your legs when you're lying on your back? Now, though, guard is my best position and I'm able to defend myself and even successfully submit people from that position. I love being on my back, as weird as that sounds, and this change in mentality is the same one that Barbara was encouraging me to see with the protective position. It's not about labeling positions or feelings as weak or strong, right or wrong; for me, it's about learning to be strong in a protective position instead of being weak and afraid. I realized that I already learned this lesson with jiu-jitsu and the guard position – I took what's seen as a weak and vulnerable position to the average person and turned it into one of my strengths (to be fair, it's not like I created the concept of guard attacks. They're a very common part of jiu-jitsu. I'm more talking about my mentality toward that position and my

111

personal ability to attack from there.).

While the lesson that I learned was unique to me and I'm not saying that everyone who participates in dance-movement therapy will investigate the exact same strength and weakness spectrum, I wanted to tell this story to emphasize how much can be revealed when you start listening to your body. I started the session saying that my shoulder was sore and ended with a new perspective on strength in protective positions. I'll finish my reflection of my experience with another sports metaphor to give you some advice as to how to listen to your body so you can experience the same revelations that I did. When I played soccer and basketball, I always played my best defense when I stopped thinking and solely listened to my body. I stopped trying to predict how my opponent was going to move and instead trusted my body to see what was going on and know the right decision to make. This ability to trust your body's wisdom and allow it to lead is the same thing that you need to have when you approach dance-movement therapy. It might be incredibly counterintuitive, and it might be wholly uncomfortable in the beginning, but your body has lessons to teach you if you only know how to listen.

How to Find a Dance-Movement Therapist

All dance-movement therapists are certified under the American Dance Therapy Association, and they fall under two levels of education: registered and board-certified. Registered dance-movement therapists have completed basic training, which is a Master's degree in dance-movement therapy, clinical fieldwork, and at least 700 hours of a clinical internship. Some alternative routes are available, such as obtaining a Master's degree and dance-movement therapy experience outside of the coursework. Board-certified dance-movement therapists, on the other hand, have completed 3640 hours of paid clinical practice as a registered dance-movement therapist. This means that they are at a much higher level of competency and often work in private practice. If you're looking to find a dance-movement therapist, you can visit the American Dance Therapy Association's website here: www.adta.org/find-a-dmt. While their search tool does not allow you to differentiate between levels of dance-movement therapists, the list of results shows whether the practitioner is a registered or board-certified dance-movement therapist.

Chapter 11:
Trauma-Sensitive Yoga
ೞ౫ಖ

Beyond being good for the body, yoga can be incredibly healing psychologically, as well. I was interested in scheduling some reflective time into my life, so I signed up for a traditional yoga class at my local gym. Sure, I'd experienced yoga before, usually sweating it out in a hot yoga studio for maximum calorie burning. This time, though, I wanted something calming that would allow me to connect with both my body and thoughts. When I walked in, the room was dark and silent, and I could smell essential oils in the air. Throughout the hour of the class, we moved through about five poses; the goal was to sink into the poses as deeply as we could. Oddly enough, my mental state during the class can be divided into four fifteen-minute sessions. The first fifteen minutes were spent with my mind running a million miles an hour, as it usually does. I was thinking about my to-do list, wondering what my cat was doing at home, complaining about how this certain pose made my hip hurt, and the like. The second fifteen minutes were spent berating myself for being unable to focus. The goal was to calm my mind, *god damnit*, and I was failing horribly at that. The third fifteen minutes were blissfully silent in my head. I don't know what changed (and perhaps it merely just took 30 minutes for my mind to settle down), but I was able to relax and simply *feel* what was going on in my body. The final fifteen minutes were incredibly emotional. This was the time where I was able to connect with what was going on in my soul during the class and achieve a true meditative and restorative state.

While trauma-sensitive yoga won't take the same shape as a traditional yoga class, even a restorative yoga class, it has a similar goal of connecting with your mind and body. For many trauma survivors, being conscious of the body and being present in the body is quite a challenge. Tracey, the aforementioned EMDR practitioner, explained that "for people whose body has been harmed in many ways, especially people who are sexual abuse survivors, having to focus on the body is very difficult and very scary and very triggering. They don't feel safe; they don't feel stable." Trauma-sensitive yoga attempts to make your body a safe space again by allowing you the space to relearn to trust your body and by providing you the opportunity to make choices for your body. Hilary Mueller, a therapist and trauma-sensitive yoga practitioner from St. Paul, Minnesota, elaborates on the approach, saying that trauma-sensitive yoga provides "opportunities for trauma survivors to make choices for their bodies, to be in control of how they come back into their bodies, and to learn to trust themselves that they can make decisions about what's right for their body." As trauma survivors are oftentimes disconnected from their body and have had their control and choices stripped away from them during their trauma, having the choice placed back in their hands can lead to immense healing in the self-body relationship.

The attempt to bring someone back into touch with their body during talk therapy is often ineffective. After all, sitting there talking about your body is much less powerful then moving it, feeling how it moves, and understanding and deciding what's comfortable and what isn't. "Trauma-sensitive yoga is a less threatening, less activating, and more indirect way to offer choices," Hilary said, and therefore can accomplish that goal of bodily connection and autonomy. The main focus of trauma-sensitive yoga is interoception, which is the innate ability to sense what your body feels and needs: does this feel good? Do I want more of this? Is this too much? This process of interoception is more a gut feeling than a cognitive understanding of the body's limits, and it can start to rebuild the trust and understanding between you and your body.

Trauma-sensitive yoga is not a traditional yoga practice. Each practitioner starts with the trauma-sensitive yoga principles of choice and adds a form of gentle yoga; for Hilary, this is yin yoga. "The yoga is slow. It's more of an introspective process," Hilary described. "There's also always an out." When a choice is presented to us, it's often in the form of "this" or "that". For some people, neither "this" nor "that" feels right, and they need a "neither" or "none of the above" option. Trauma-sensitive yoga includes this choice.

Participants always have the option to come out of the position or even leave the class if it doesn't feel right to them. In addition, there are always multiple modifications provided to accommodate each individual's mobility and needs, as well as their ability to make choices for themselves. Furthermore, it's emphasized that there's no right or wrong way to do a pose. In a traditional yoga class, the instructor might come around and move or adjust you. In trauma-sensitive yoga, that's not the case. "Whatever you're doing is what you should be doing," Tracey explained. "There's a lot more acceptance and understanding. We don't want people to get hurt, obviously, but it's about giving lots of modifications." Many centers that run trauma-sensitive yoga classes, such as Willow Tree Healing Center, will provide blocks, pillows, and bands to help with the modifications and make it so that everyone has the choice to participate in a way that feels good to them and their bodies.

The inclusion of choices and an opt-out acts as the bridge between trauma-sensitive yoga and a traditional yoga class. In a traditional yoga class, there's a structure and a flow, as well as a right and a wrong way to do the poses, as I discussed. An emphasis is placed on flexibility, strength, and holding the poses. In trauma-sensitive yoga, the emphasis is placed on noticing what's going on in your body and making decisions based on that information. In fact, in Hilary's trauma-sensitive yoga classes, she calls the positions "forms" instead of "poses". "'Forms' is less of an expectation," Hilary explained. "If I said to you, 'Get into child's pose', you're like–" She proceeded to break off and dramatically demonstrate contorting one's body into child's pose using an effective amount of grunts to showcase the forceful nature of it. Yes, we both laughed. You can ask me for the interview recording if you don't believe me or if you really want to hear it for yourself. "But if I say, 'We're moving into this form where your arms are here, or you could do this, or you have an option for this. Just kind of feel what feels right for your body,' there isn't that expectation of 'I gotta just do it!'" In some traumatic circumstances, such as abusive relationships, submitting to the perceived expectations can be a trauma adaptation mechanism. Trauma-sensitive yoga removes that expectation through the inclusion of choices, both to do the form or not to do the form, but also in how you do the form. The invitation is to feel what feels right to you instead of forcing yourself to fit the expectations of your environment.

As I discussed in the meditation chapter and the note about using a mental health professional in your healing journey, meditative states can be scary for many trauma survivors because of their intense hypervigilance. Shutting their eyes, being still, and turning inward makes it impossible for them to be aware of the dangers and threats in the world, and it can even cause dissociative states in some individuals. Trauma-sensitive yoga can act as a first step toward mindfulness for trauma survivors. "It's a way for them to approach [mindfulness], but also knowing that they can come out of it whenever they want," Hilary explained. The non-directive nature of trauma-sensitive yoga allows for each individual to be where they are in their healing process without forcing them to take steps or enter spaces that are not safe for them yet.

Trauma-sensitive yoga also acts as a way for

individuals to work through the freeze response that's so common in trauma survivors. A trauma-sensitive yoga class provides the opportunity to freeze, recognize what's happening in your brain, and work through it to remind yourself that you're safe. Neurobiologically, it moves the emphasis from the trauma-activated brainstem to the cortex of your brain, where logic and higher powers of reasoning reside. It's there where you're able to talk yourself down from that freeze response, recognize that you have a choice, and decide how to proceed from there. Going through this process can actually rewire your brain so your automatic reaction is no longer to freeze, but to think and respond to the situation.

Logistically, trauma-sensitive yoga is offered in a small-group setting (don't worry, though – there are one-on-one options for trauma-sensitive yoga. Ask your therapist or trauma-sensitive yoga practitioner if that's something you'd be more comfortable with.) and usually runs in multi-week cycles. Some individuals choose to take multiple cycles of trauma-sensitive yoga, whereas others feel they've gotten the healing they need from just one session. The room in which the class is held is kept less stimulating than a traditional yoga studio because the scents and sounds of a traditional yoga studio can range from uncomfortable to triggering for many trauma survivors. Furthermore, many of the elements of the studio are kept the same week to week to create predictability for the attendees. For example, Hilary explained that the music she plays and the arrangement of the room is the same every week, and she even wears the same outfit for every class.

How to Find a Trauma-Sensitive Yoga Practitioner

Finding a trauma-sensitive yoga practitioner can be somewhat difficult, depending on how you approach it. There's two parts to the name: "trauma" and "yoga". If you start with the "yoga" piece and try to find a trauma-sensitive class in a traditional yoga studio, you can't be certain that the individual instructing that class has had mental health training and will be able to preserve the specific trauma-sensitive nature of the program. If you start with the "trauma" piece, though, then you're much more likely to find a class with a trained instructor. While there are many certifying organizations, the term "Trauma-Sensitive Yoga" was coined by The Trauma Center in Massachusetts. A list of trauma-sensitive yoga practitioners trained by The Trauma Center can be found at www.traumasensitiveyoga.com/find-a-facilitator.html.

There's no blanket statement that I can make that says that only these types of individuals are qualified to practice trauma-sensitive yoga; for example, someone who isn't trained by The Trauma Center might be great at practicing trauma-sensitive yoga because of outside education and personal experience with trauma. Unfortunately, that's not always the case, and my priority is to keep your best interest and your safety in mind. Therefore, I highly recommend that you consult the list provided at the link above before reaching out to yoga studios that offer trauma-sensitive classes. There are trained practitioners all over the globe, so you shouldn't be limited in finding a certified trauma-sensitive yoga practitioner near you.

If you're uncertain whether a local yoga studio offers qualified trauma-sensitive yoga, look closely at the name of their classes. Trauma-sensitive yoga, while the common term for the practice, is actually specific to programs at or programs taught by individuals instructed at The Trauma Center. If the class is called something like "Yoga For Healing Trauma", which is what Hilary calls her classes (don't worry – she's trained in trauma-sensitive yoga, though from another institution, and she has an extensive background in mental healthcare), then it's likely not conducted by someone trained by The Trauma Center, and it warrants more investigation into the practitioner's qualifications.

A Note About General Exercise

Exercise is often the key ingredient to good physical and mental health, but despite that, it may not be the best fit for trauma survivors. Exercise can be helpful for letting pent-up energy out of the body, but certain forms of it can mimic the flight response. The adrenaline dump you get from, say, running is the same adrenaline dump you got during your traumatic event. If you're aware of the similarities, though, then exercise can be safer mentally for you. That being said, activities that are grounded, such as weightlifting or even vacuuming, help you center your body and calm your nervous system. Activities that are also rhythmic and repetitive, such as running, can be soothing, too. But wait – didn't I just say that running can mimic the adrenaline dump from a fight? Yes – which is why it's important to listen to your body and understand the difference in emotions between running and fighting for your life.

More importantly than a rigid exercise routine is overall wellness. When you're healing, it's important for you to get enough sleep every night, eat a healthy diet, refrain from substance use, and, yes, move your body in a way that's healthy for you. This doesn't mean that you need to be the flawless, perfect picture of healthy living. It's simply that, when you do these things, you will feel better, you'll have more energy, and your overall wellness will improve. It's not that exercise is a prescription for healing from trauma; it's that general wellness is a model for an overall good life.

Therefore, when you're considering the exercise you're undertaking during your healing journey (and, really, in everyday life), you need to ask yourself if it's adding to your overall health. Is it helping you manage your symptoms, or is it a way to punish yourself for the guilt you feel surrounding your trauma? Is it a way for you to feel free and powerful, or are you a slave to the expectations you set for yourself? As with many other methods of "at-home" healing, such as meditation and spending regular time in nature, if it's working for you, then keep doing it. If it's not, switch it up.

Chapter 12:
Equine-Assisted Therapy

ೞ൸

Horses are incredible, intuitive, and almost magical beings, so it's no surprise that they're capable of having a healing hand in the life of someone who experienced a traumatic incident. Briefly, equine-assisted therapy for traumatic situations is the use of horses and horse interactions to re-position one's perspective of the trauma that they went through, whether these new perspectives come from an interaction between you and a horse or from viewing and identifying with an interaction between two horses. The majority of equine-assisted therapy is practiced under EAGALA-certified practitioners, so before we dive into the meat of equine-assisted therapy, let's discuss what that governing body is all about, as their mission is the foundation of equine-assisted therapy.

Equine Assisted Growth and Learning Association (EAGALA)

EAGALA stands for the Equine Assisted Growth and Learning Association, but it's most commonly known by the acronym, which is pronounced ee-gala. It was founded as a non-profit in 1999 and was one of the first organizations to develop standards for the incorporation of horses into mental health care. Now, EAGALA operates in 45 countries and served over 60,000 clients in 2018.

As far as the human counterpart, both equine specialists and mental health practitioners can be certified in the EAGALA model, and both types of professionals are critical in the equine-assisted therapy process. EAGALA describes the equine-assisted therapy process and their model as a "hands-on approach where clients are given the space to project and analyze their situations, make connections, and find their own solutions", which results in longer and deeper connections and associations.

Their model has four tenets: a team approach, sessions entirely on the ground, a solution-focused approach, and an adherence to the EAGALA code of ethics. This means that the horse, the professionals on site, and you are all team members in the therapeutic process; that no riding is incorporated into the therapeutic process; that the sessions are focused on finding a path to healing instead of beating the current issues to death; and that all sessions and all members of the process adhere to professionalism, confidence, respect, and honesty. Most importantly, it's guided entirely by the you, the client – what you need and at the pace you want to work. It is also incredibly powerful because it allows the human professionals to get out of the way. Well-meaning people can say things that result in unintended effects, and those effects can cause a hindrance in the healing process or even cause you to not return.

Why Horses?

As I said, horses are beautiful and somewhat mystical, but why are they so beneficial in the trauma healing process? First and foremost, horses don't store trauma like humans do. Heather Jeffrey, the COO of Acres for Life, an equine-assisted therapy center in Minnesota, says that horses are "different with their interactions with trauma. They are both grounded and hypervigilant at the same time. Horses are a different kind of animal, and there's a lot that you can learn from them." This comes from the fact that they are prey animals, as opposed to predators, like dogs (though dogs can be helpful in their own way during your healing journey, as I'll discuss in the next chapter). "Horses can mirror what healthy awareness looks like, as opposed to hypervigilance, which takes over everything," Heather added. "They are aware, they are in relationship with others, and they are able to be grounded and breathe." Therefore, horses can serve as a role model for trauma survivors, a role model that recognizes a fear response and a tendency to be hypervigilant, but also one that demonstrates being grounded and holding positive relationships.

When you're working with horses, there's no judgement, no expectations, and no agenda. The lack of these aspects that are prevalent in many human interactions contributes to creating a safe space where you can feel at ease opening up about your experiences and working through them. Even more importantly (as this is a common worry when working with human mental health professionals), horses don't tell secrets, so you can count on 100% confidentiality from them. Partly because of those characteristics and partly because of their ability to be unapologetically themselves, horses are more equipped to break into therapeutic relationships. For example, Sally told a story of a client who was extremely closed off until they went outside, and a horse walked by and very obviously passed gas. The client started laughing, which essentially broke the ice and allowed for the therapeutic process to begin. Horses are able to break down walls in their own unique way.

Horses are also incredibly in-tune to what's going on internally with the client. They know when to move closer, when to move away, and how to interact with each individual client on a level that is nearly impossible for humans to understand. This allows for the equine specialists and mental health professionals to take a backseat and allow the horse to play a prominent symbolic role in the movie of the client's healing. This awareness on the horse's part comes from their life as a prey animal. Every day, they need to be aware of their surroundings on an incredibly detailed level to identify any threats, and they look at things like body language and tension in the air to do so. These skills help them read and relate to people on a level that few other animals can.

Finally, horses are *big*. Being able to interact with animals who are potentially ten times larger than you can be incredibly empowering for people, especially individuals who have never interacted with horses before. It can also serve as a challenge to overcome for individuals who are scared of horses. As I said, they're big, and if you've never stood next to an animal of that size and that strength, it can be a bit intimidating. Overcoming that fear and building a trusting relationship with such a large animal can be very helpful in building self-confidence and healing from trauma.

What Occurs During EAT

At an equine-assisted therapy session, you'll have two professionals with you: a mental health practitioner, who is responsible for caring for your emotional safety, creating the therapeutic plan, and ensuring ethical practice; and an equine specialist, who manages physical safety of both you and the horse, collaborates with the mental health practitioner in creating the therapeutic plan, and comments accurately on the horse's behavior.

Equine-assisted therapy under the EAGALA model is completely on the ground, meaning you will never ride the horse. This increases accessibility to equine-assisted therapy by opening the doors to individuals who have no equine experience, who are fearful of riding a horse, or who are physically unable to. It also removes an element of control from the session. When you're riding a horse, you are in control of it. You tell it where to go, what to do, and how fast to move. When horses become symbols in your story, as they do during the equine-assisted therapy process, though, it becomes difficult to apply control. For example, if you resonate with a horse and see that horse as yourself, would you feel free and healed if someone put a bridle in your mouth and told you what to do? What if, alternatively, one horse represents your trauma? As Sally put it, "you don't want to saddle up Trauma and take it for a ride."

Having the interactions on the ground with the horses free to do what they want also accurately represents your ability to control various aspects of your life. You and the horse are both able to move closer or away from each other, for example, which can help you in your symbolic journey. Sticking with the previous example, when you are physically able to move yourself away from Trauma (in this case, a horse that symbolizes trauma), you can feel the same effect inside your own mind and soul of you moving away from your traumatic incident. As another example, if you identify a horse as yourself and see it get bit by another horse, you can physically move that horse to a safe place, which symbolically moves you to a safe place. Perhaps you weren't able to do that in real life, so having the equine interactions play out with you as director can initiate symbolic change, which then can turn into realized change in your own life.

During a course of equine-assisted therapy, there are four categories for structuring sessions, and Lynn Moore, the aforementioned founder of Acres for Life, was kind enough to walk me through them. The first category is observation. You would spend time discussing what you see when you observe the field of horses – does one horse represent courage? Does one represent addiction? This allows you start understanding the layout of your story. The second category is relationships.

This could be your relationship with yourself, your relationship with others, your relationship with your job, your relationship with the environment – whatever relationship comes up most strongly for you. The third category revolves around the presence or absence of movement. If you're feeling stuck in your trauma or in a negative relationship, being able to move the horses and props around could simulate the movement you need in your life. Conversely, if you feel like everything is moving too quickly, being able to still the scene and calm it down could help you begin to find that peace and stillness in your own life. The fourth and final category is that of creation. When you're ready to step into your recovery, your session would be structured around you using the props, horses, and the environment to create what you want your recovered life and recovery process to look like. Through the process and throughout moving through these four categories, a deep sense of awareness of self and situation comes, which is critical in your healing process.

Mounted Equine-Assisted Therapy: An Alternative to EAGALA

While the EAGALA model is the most commonly practiced method of equine-assisted therapy, there is an alternative in the Epona program. This form of equine-assisted therapy is named after the ancient horse goddess Epona, who was a symbol of healing, balance, and transformation in Celtic culture. Founded by Linda Kohanov in 1997, the Epona model of equine-assisted therapy and equine-facilitated learning

129

address all types of disorders, from physical to occupational disorders. Linda describes the model as creating a place for survivors to "explore assertiveness, stress reduction, and emotional fitness skills, strengthening self-esteem and personal empowerment in the process." Alongside equine interaction and general husbandry skills, Epona sessions can also incorporate meditation, journaling, and the creative arts.

Molly DePrekel is an Epona-certified practitioner and therapist from Minnesota, and she was kind enough to walk me through what she does during her brand of equine-assisted therapy. Her sessions include a variety of groundwork and riding activities, depending on the needs of the client, including conscious grooming activities (this could be a great mindfulness opportunity), walking with the horse, Tellington TTouch (a form of bodywork that consists of circular touches on the body of the animal), movement – including yoga and stretching – with the horse, and riding activities. These riding activities are not generally what you'd think of when you think of horseback riding – jumping, galloping across the field, and the like. The activities in the Epona model are more therapeutic and concentrate more heavily on feeling the horse beneath you. For example, you might lie down on the back of the horse with your head on its rump, feel the horse underneath you, and concentrate on your breath, allowing you to calm, self-regulate, and release your trauma. The openness of that position or the act of the horse moving underneath you might be too uncomfortable for you, so the therapist might instruct you to sit strong and tall on a stationary horse. While these are just two examples of the mounted activities within the Epona model, they help explain the type of riding activities that can be done.

Why, though, after I spent a fair amount of words discussing why equine-assisted therapy is solely groundwork, would I bring up a method that incorporates riding? Molly explained that the more she works with trauma, the more she realizes how critical movement is in the healing process, and many other mental health practitioners and trauma research studies agree with her. For some people, getting on the horse, feeling their whole body and the body of the horse, and trying something new is healing and empowering, and it's a new method of movement that can allow the trauma to release from your body. As far as safety concerns, an animal handler will always be present if riding is incorporated into the session.

Regardless of whether the therapy takes place on the ground or on the back of the horse, the Epona model is centered around having calm and safe experiences with the horses and learning to become aware and process the information that you're receiving through your senses. When you have an interaction with the horse, whether that's grooming it or performing TTouch on it, you will be encouraged to take note of how you feel, how you make the horse feel, and how the horse makes you feel. This consciousness in the present moment is the first step toward self-regulation. Furthermore, recognizing those feelings of calm, peace, and safety, and storing them away in your body to revisit during times of stress is an incredibly powerful sensorimotor marker. Some clients will further mark the moment by photographing or taking a video of themselves and the horse. This enables the benefits of equine-assisted therapy to reach far beyond the session.

Another goal of the Epona model is to teach you how to be assertive and set boundaries with the horses. Oftentimes in trauma, boundaries and assertiveness were either not allowed or completely obliterated, leaving you feeling powerless. Working with a horse, who is much larger and much more powerful than you, and being able to give it directions – that it follows – can be quite empowering and help you learn to reform those boundaries and reassert yourself in your daily life. Molly's slogan that she tells clients is that if "you can move a 1,000-pound animal and calm it down, you can absolutely do that for yourself." She said – and I believe – that that revelation has been a lightbulb moment for many of her clients.

Though the client is the focus of the session, the horses are incredibly well-cared for, as well. They are not just tools, but active partners, in the Epona model, just as they are in the EAGALA model. They expect a certain level of care in exchange for their hard work, and a unique way that Molly's clients care for the horses after the sessions is wiping them down with their hands. Horses are incredibly aware of emotions and transfers of energy, and the purpose of wiping down the horse with your hands after the session is to remove any trauma that you may have released that stuck to the horse. There's no point to you releasing your trauma only for it to enter the horse, and this closing activity at the end of sessions prevents that from happening and allows you to thank the horse for their service.

Benefits of EAT

While there's not extensive research on the benefits of

equine-assisted therapy for adults healing from trauma, a powerful study by Earles, Vernon, and Yetz found that individuals who partook in only six sessions – twelve hours – of equine-assisted therapy experienced a decrease in depression and PTSD symptoms, a less severe emotional response to trauma, less alcohol use, and an increase in the use of mindfulness strategies. In other words, the survivors who experienced equine-assisted therapy started reacting less strongly to their trauma and turned from harmful coping methods, such as alcohol use, to productive healing methods, such as mindfulness.

Anecdotally, there are many success stories of individuals healing through equine-assisted therapy. One man who attended Acres for Life didn't speak for five sessions, but when he saw a horse standing in a field with his mouth open, he related to the horse and opened up to the practitioners. He explained that he felt like that horse because he was trying to get his words, his story, and his trauma to come out but couldn't. Another woman was interacting with a horse when he put his mouth around her arm gently, walked in a large circle, put his mouth around her arm firmly, walked around in a circle again, and then bit her arm. She described these interactions as cute, then love, then pain, and used that interaction to open up about her abusive relationship. For another example, a man who attended sessions at Acres for Life had the same horse come up and put his nose over his heart every day for weeks but didn't know what that interaction meant. He finally realized that the horse was his father, who had passed away, speaking to him and telling him that it was okay to move on.

Yet another story involves a woman who identified one horse as herself and one as her PTSD. She and the horse she identified as herself shared a moment with their faces very close together, and she described it as breathing in herself again. The horse she identified as PTSD went to nip her, and she told it loudly and firmly to back off, effectively and symbolically standing up to her PTSD. These two moments chartered her healing journey.

These stories are incredibly powerful, and equine-assisted therapy could be the interaction you need to write your own breakthrough story. Because of the depth of emotion and connection created through equine-assisted therapy, the breakthroughs you have stick with you. The woman who faced off against her PTSD will remember that moment and find strength from it for months and years to come.

Even further, equine-assisted therapy differs from traditional talk therapy in two key ways. Firstly, during traditional talk therapy, there are instructions and cognitive breakthroughs; with equine-assisted therapy, there is action, movement, and physical change, all of which are guided by you as the author of your own story. Secondly, equine-assisted therapy involves *all* your senses, and because trauma is something that affects you through all sensory inputs, equine-assisted therapy is able to pull at all effects of that trauma. Sally described this relationship as "two things coming into the boxing ring that are a good match, because your senses just come alive. You're stepping into that experience, so the horrible experience of trauma can be faced head-on by this experience." I don't know about you, but I'd prefer to tackle trauma from all angles and all senses, instead of simply sitting and talking about it.

Can I Hang Out with Horses Recreationally and Get the Same Benefit?

For anyone who has interacted with horses on recreational level, it's obvious that there's something calming and peaceful about their presence. Therefore, you might be thinking that you can just go spend some time with horses and call it "equine-assisted therapy"; that is not the case. The EAGALA model is built on a four-legged stool, meaning that the survivor and the horse play a critical role, but so do the equine specialist and the mental health practitioner. Without the professionals on site, there's not only a risk to the physical and emotional safety of the horses and the survivor, but a lack of a healing setting.

Being in nature on an equine-assisted therapy facility brings with it a certain atmosphere that's not found in common barn settings. The mental health professionals are there to be backseat holders of your story, as Sally put it, and give you the tools and environment to breathe life back into your story. That environment and the combination of the horses and the nature create a safe space for you to open up about your trauma and sort through the messiness that lies below. "[Clients] feel loved, held, and accepted," explained Sally when asked about the environment at equine-assisted therapy. While the horses are an incredibly important part of that (Sally described them as "the leading catalyst"), the mental health professionals and equine specialists play key roles in creating that environment.

My Experience with EAT

After interviewing Heather, Lynn, and Sally, I asked them what I missed from our interview – what other questions I should be asking, which other professionals I should be interviewing, and what other topics I should be exploring. Lynn told me to experience equine-assisted therapy for myself, so she and Heather invited me back for a quick personal development session so I could see firsthand the power of it. I went into the session a little nervous and a lot excited, and my expectations were wide open. I didn't have anything in particular that I wanted to talk about, but we all agreed that something would come up.

I started out by observing the two fields of horses, and Heather and Lynn asked me what stood out to me. I saw two horses lying down in the snow on their side, and that reminded me of a memory from my childhood where I saw two sheep doing the same thing. We moved into one of the pastures, and I went around and said hello to all of the horses. Being out there, with the horses and in nature, really brought up the theme of memories: the memory of my horsepack trip in British Columbia for my tenth birthday, trekking with the Exmoor ponies while at vet school in Edinburgh, and many more from the course of my life. This introduced the concept of symbolism that is so prevalent in equine-assisted therapy. The horses served as a symbol for my place in the world, the social interactions between the horses served as a symbol for the type of relationships I'd like to have with people, and the whole scene of the horses and nature served as a symbol for how I wanted my life to look.

Because of the links between the scene in front of me and my childhood memories, I began to think about the definition of progress. Oftentimes, progress is considered moving forward, and regression is considered moving backwards. Since all of these memories of my childhood were coming up and contrasting with feelings of being stuck in the city and being surrounded by gray, it cemented my desire to return to the area of the world I was raised in, spend more time with my family, and dig deeper into my roots in the natural world. That challenged my idea of progress, as, like I said – progress, traditionally, is moving forward and leaving everything behind you, well, *behind.*

After I had the progress discussion with Heather and Lynn, the discussion transitioned into other areas of life. What represented home and what didn't represent home? How do I honor my authentic self and my true desires at this transition point in my life? Where would I put myself in the scene that I see in front of me? When they asked me that last question, I pointed to an area of unmarked snow that was further down by the edge of the pasture. Just beyond the fence was a small grove of trees, and the sun was filtering through the branches and lighting up that area of untouched snow. I said I would like to be there.

The question they asked me next honestly redefined how I approached all the choices I've made since that moment: "What's stopping you?" I realized that I had been asking permission – Can we go in the horse pasture? Can I go say hi to everyone? – instead of treating it like it was my session, as Heather and Lynn had told me to do. So, I went down into that untracked area of snow, plopped down on my back, closed my eyes, and just breathed. I listened to the sound of the birds and the occasional horse whinny, and I appreciated the silence and the lack of cars as background noise. Eventually, I made a snow angel and traipsed around to find leaves to build a crown for it.

That simple act of lying down in the snow, building a snow angel, and being surrounded by nature and the horses really symbolized who I am working to become. My ideal self and my ideal life take place in the country, in the peace, with the freedom to go lie in the snow for 20 minutes if that's what's going to make my heart happy. It involves being surrounded by my animals and does not include the pressure to be someone I'm not or please others at the expense of myself. That simple little snow angel was both a slap in the face and a wake-up call, and that really sealed the deal for me that equine-assisted therapy was powerful work. Yes, we talked some, but it was conversational instead of traditional talk therapy. Yes, they asked me some directive questions, but the majority of the session was me appreciating being outdoors and following the symbolic path of where I was going in life through that session.

Overall, my experience with equine-assisted therapy showed me the depth and amount of symbolism that takes place during the sessions. I understood on an academic level the importance of moving the horses and props to set a scene and envisioning your life's story with the backdrop of the facility, but I didn't understand the depth of the symbolism that occurs when you immerse yourself in that environment and allow yourself to flow with what you're feeling. I had my unique lessons that were learned, both about myself and the direction my life was going to take, and you'll experience your own lessons that are different than mine but perfect for you. All I can say after experiencing equine-assisted therapy is that I was rejuvenated, empowered, and motivated; imagine what multiple sessions could do for you in your trauma healing process.

Finding an Equine-Assisted Therapy Practitioner

In order to find an equine-assisted therapy practitioner, you need to determine which method of equine-assisted therapy (EAGALA or Epona) is right for you. If you've chosen to pursue EAGALA-based therapy, then visit www.eagala.org/programs. You can search by location for EAGALA-certified practitioners and facilities, and you can specify whether you'd like the facility to have extra experience with and resources for veterans. If you've chosen to pursue Epona-based therapy, then visit eponaquest.com/recommended-instructors/. Here, you can sort recommended practitioners by US geographical region and by continent. "Recommended practitioners" are those who have completed the Epona apprenticeship, a 36-day program. Epona practitioners are not necessarily certified mental health practitioners, but there is a list of acronyms on the Epona webpage listed above that explain each practitioner's additional qualifications. When choosing an Epona practitioner for trauma healing, I'd focus on the ones that have CEFIP (Certified Equine Facilitated Interaction Professionals, in mental health or education), EFMHA (Equine Facilitated Mental Health Association), or, preferably, EFP (Equine Facilitated Psychotherapy) next to their names. As with all individuals you want to work with on a professional level during your healing journey, investigate their credentials and make sure that they are qualified and certified to help you heal from trauma.

Chapter 13:
Canine-Assisted Therapy

Cଅଌଅ

I don't know about you, but I've seen and experienced therapy dogs in my everyday life. The University of Minnesota has a program where they bring therapy dogs into the on-campus clinic and the recreation center during the week for faculty, staff, and students to visit, pet, and de-stress with. I used this service on many occasions before I had pets of my own, both to get my puppy snuggle fix and to reap the benefits of therapy dogs.

Now that I have a pup of my own, she's become an emotional support pillar for me. She's not trained as a therapy dog (and I'll discuss the differences between different types of working dogs below), but simply being around her helps me feel better and stay calmer. Plus, her crawling into my lap to lick away my tears when I cry doesn't hurt, either! If you have dogs, I'm sure you wouldn't disagree that they're very beneficial for health, so it's no surprise that dogs are a great animal for animal-assisted therapy.

The Use of Dogs in Trauma Therapy

Molly DePrekel, the previously mentioned Epona equine-assisted therapy practitioner and a mental health professional at the Midwest Center for Trauma and Emotional Healing in Minnetonka, Minnesota, works with her dog, Willow, during her counseling sessions. Interactions with Willow – and therapy dogs in general – aid clients in opening up about their story. For example, Molly had one client come in who wasn't in line with themselves and their emotions, and the client sat down next to Willow on the couch. Willow immediately jumped off the couch away from that person, causing the client to laugh, then start to open up about their story. Willow then returned to the couch and remained next to the client. This just goes to show how attuned to the state of the client the therapy dog is.

During trauma counseling, it's important not to have the client open up immediately about their traumatic event, as that can cause them to re-imprint with the event. Therapy dogs can be used in this instance to redirect the client. This could take the form of petting the dog, taking the dog for a walk outside, practicing TTouch on it, teaching the dog tricks, or simply breathing with it. All of these activities are designed to allow the client to open up about their trauma but in a manner that is controlled, paced, and aided with the comforting (and sometimes comic!) presence of a therapy dog.

ESA vs. Therapy Dog vs. Service Dog

The distinctions between an emotional support animal (ESA), a therapy dog, and a service dog can sometimes become muddled, especially with all the media attention surrounding ESAs and with all the people who have a form of working dog. Most of the dogs that you'll encounter in a therapeutic practice are therapy dogs, but it's important to understand how all three work and the legislation surrounding them so you understand who you're really working with.

Emotional Support Animal

An ESA is a pet whose presence helps you feel better. There is no formal training nor official documentation for ESAs, and ESAs can be any type of animal (yes, miniature ponies have been ESAs). ESAs do not have access to all public spaces, like service dogs do, though they are allowed in the cabins of airplanes and in all federal housing with a letter from your doctor stating your need for an ESA. Much of the controversy surrounding ESAs arises from the multitude of online organizations selling ESA "registrations", patches, harnesses, certificates, and more. While it may seem tempting to call your dog an ESA, buy them a fancy harness, and go live life with them, the only thing that is actually required (and legally allowed) is a letter from your doctor. They don't need to wear a patch. They don't need to be registered with an organization. You only need to have a letter from your doctor stating that you need an ESA that you can show to airlines and landlords.

Therapy Dog

A therapy dog is a dog that has undergone a training program and is registered with their program. There is no such thing as a *certified* therapy dog, as there are many bodies that provide training and registration for therapy dogs. Pet Partners is a common organization for the training of both therapy dogs and humans, though many local dog training clubs offer therapy dog classes. Therapy dogs do not have unlimited access to public spaces, either. They're often used in nursing homes or mental health facilities to aid in the therapeutic process and to bring comfort.

Service Dogs

Service dogs are trained to provide a specific service to one person with a disability. For someone suffering from a traumatic experience, this could mean alerting the handler to when their emotions are getting out of hand or waking them up from a nightmare. Service dogs can be trained by the handler or by an outside organization. That being said, it's not necessarily the best idea to pick a puppy up and say you'll train it to be service dog when you're healing yourself. While training and handling a dog can be rewarding and healthy for some people, others, who are not as stable with their emotions, can have their instability rub off on the dog during its critical learning time and damage it for life. Furthermore, training a service dog can take multiple years, so it's not a commitment to take lightly. If you do decide to train your own service dog, Molly and I would both highly recommend seeking the help and direction of a professional trainer. To be clear, I'm not saying that those healing from trauma should not *own* a service dog; it might just be a better idea to get an *already trained, adult* dog from a training organization.

All service dogs are protected under the Americans with Disabilities Act, and they're allowed to go anywhere that their handler is allowed to go. The only reason they may be removed from a space is if they are dangerous, out of control, or not potty trained. They are not required to wear any sort of identification, though most handlers have a vest on them that identifies them as a service or working dog. They also do not have to be registered under any body, which might come as a surprise. Generally, they are not considered pets, but working animals, though they are with their handlers 100% of the time.

Which type of dog should I work with?

This is really a question for your mental health practitioner or your therapist. If you're working with a dog in the office (meaning you are not its handler), then you'll likely be working with a trained therapy dog. If you're looking to bring a dog into your own life, then it's worth further exploring the training requirements and legislation surrounding each type of working dog. Make sure to also discuss with your therapist which type of working dog is best for you or if you should even consider bringing a dog into your home in the first place.

Why are Dogs Ideal for Trauma Healing?

As I said in the beginning, it's somewhat intuitive that dogs are beneficial to our emotions and stress levels, and if you have dogs of your own, you can probably attest to this on a personal level. Beyond that, though, dogs are uniquely suited to this type of therapy work because of a variety of characteristics. In terms of a therapist working with their therapy dog in an office setting, dogs are much easier to take back and forth from home to work with you. You can take cats, but that's highly dependent on whether they're amenable to car rides. People are also more commonly allergic to cats, and the last thing you'd want is to walk into your therapist's office and walk out with an EpiPen in your thigh. Dogs are also much easier to train than cats; whereas cats kind of do whatever they want, you can train a dog to relate to clients and behave in a constructive manner.

In terms of the benefits of dogs to the client, dogs are uniquely able to help calm people down and get rid of nerves. They're also easier to relate to. If you're anything like me, you say hi to the pups at a party before the people, and by about three hours in, you're off in the corner snuggling the dog rather than speaking with the people (only me? Wow...). In addition, you can bring dogs out into nature, so you can reap the benefits of spending time with dogs *and* being in nature.

Dogs, specifically owning them, have physical health benefits, as well. Their presence and caring for them lowers blood pressure in response to stress, and building a connection with them is connected to long-term stability and health. They also encourage us to exercise, which comes with its own immense set of health benefits, and they can serve as an antidote to loneliness, worry, anxiety, and pain. It is perhaps because of these physical benefits that a study in Austria and Germany reported $386 million in savings per year from pet owners because of decreased doctor visits. Canine interactions can potentially be the first step toward solving the trauma economic crisis (somewhat joking, but also serious)!

Where to Find Therapy Dogs

If you've decided you could benefit from canine-assisted therapy or would like to give it a shot, a simple Google search for "canine-assisted therapy near me" or "therapy dogs near me" should return quite a lot of results for you to sort through. Some will undoubtedly be places that train therapy dogs, but it's a good place to start. The American Kennel Club also has a list of registered therapy dog organizations and the state and city they are in, which can be found at www.akc.org/sports/title-recognition-program/therapy-dog-program/therapy-dog-organizations. This is not an exhaustive list by any means, but it's quite an extensive one and another great place to start. Finally, asking your current therapist or calling a local therapist and asking if they know of any canine-assisted therapy programs in the area is a great last resort.

Chapter 14:
Ecotherapy and
Nature-Based Therapies

೧೪ೀ

Nature. That beautiful, wonderful, completely magical world that sits just outside our windows and just beyond the city boundaries. I and many others have reported immense benefits from being in nature, including things like "feeling refreshed" and "feeling at peace". It's nearly impossible to describe these feelings adequately with words, though. How do you explain the tears streaming down your face when you're watching the sun set over the ocean? How do you describe the feeling of greatness and the feeling of smallness when you're surrounded by hundred-year-old redwoods? How do you tell someone that the soaring cliffs know *exactly how you feel* as you're delving into your trauma? You can't put it into words. You can't say that you feel at peace, inspired, understood, or any of those words, but that's not what's important. What's important is that nature can give us that feeling and that healing, whether we understand or can describe it or not. Some of the most dramatic elements of nature, such as cliffs, giant trees, and roaring rivers, can be perfect reflections of the emotions in our own lives as we heal from trauma, reflections that you wouldn't be able to find anywhere else, especially not in a therapist's office. You can go out in the wilderness and scream with the river, ground yourself like the trees, and cry with the cliffs; you can let loose without any fear of scaring a therapist or being judged by whoever you're speaking to. Nature has the power to heal woven into every fiber of its being, power that is both backed by research and by the personal and unexplainable experience that we have when we're outdoors.

Health Benefits of Nature

Beyond giving us all the good feels, nature provides a host of well-documented and empirically-studied health benefits. Physiologically, a meta-analysis by Twohig-Bennet and Jones in 2018 showed that time spent in nature caused decreases in heart rate, salivary cortisol levels, blood pressure, and cholesterol and decreases in the risk for type II diabetes, cardiovascular diseases, and all-around mortality. In addition, rates of stroke and asthma were decreased with an increased exposure to nature. Frumkin et al. concluded similar results from their study in 2017, stating that contact with nature helped address cardiovascular disease and obesity. Those are awesome side effects of being in nature, especially when we keep in mind the ACEs study and the huge variety of negative physical health outcomes that can form from childhood trauma. In other words, time spent in nature can address the physical health problems that arise from trauma, as well as the mental health struggles that are more directly tied to the trauma.

The mind and soul benefits of nature are immense, and when healing from a psychological trauma, it's as important – or even more important – to consider this collection of benefits, too. In 2014, Beyer (Kirsten M. Beyer, not me!) et al. took the widespread knowledge that nature helps with recovery from mental fatigue and reduces stress, examined it further, and found that time spent in nature resulted in a reduction of symptoms accompanying depression and anxiety. Other mental health benefits include attention restoration and the evocation of positive emotions, as found by Abraham, Sommerhalder, and Abel in 2009, and the relaxation of the senses, the infusion of fresh energy into our bodies, and an increase in self-concept, self-confidence, and feelings of self-worth, which Morris discussed in her 2003 literature review.

Why is this the case? What is so special about nature that it seems to heal almost anything that ails us? From a physiological perspective, Amy Sugeno, an ecotherapist from Marble Falls, Texas, explained that time spent in nature results in passive relaxation on the nervous system and regulation of cortisol and cortisol patterns, which help explain the mental health benefits that occur. Furthermore, there are four specific qualities of nature that cause a restorative environment, and therefore, the observed positive effects: "being away", extent, fascination, and compatibility. Nature, by default, is separate from the downtown busyness of life and, when we spend time in it, we give ourselves time to "be away" from whatever stresses from daily life are weighing on us – including the emotions and struggles surrounding a traumatic experience. Nature is also extensive, meaning that it spans a time and space that can be incomprehensible to us, as we live relatively short lifespans. It in itself is something bigger and something more than us, which can allow us to connect to something greater than ourselves, a connection that can lead to inner peace and restoration. In addition, nature pulls at our involuntary attention and causes fascination. We don't have to concentrate on appreciating a beautiful sunset; we just know that it's beautiful, and it seeps into our souls without our trying. This allows our voluntary attention – the one that can often be depleted by all the demands of everyday life – to relax and recuperate. Finally, there is some part of nature that is compatible with everyone. Whether you feel more at home surrounded by 14,000ft peaks or in your local park, there is a place for you in nature. These four characteristics of the greenery in our world cause it to have restorative properties and lead to the health benefits that it so regularly causes.

What You Need from Nature in Order to Heal

While these health benefits are amazing, it's important to understand what you need from nature on a personal level. Just as a cancer patient has medical and healing needs, you, as a trauma survivor, do, as well. Before I get into exactly how to reap these benefits using nature-based therapy, you need to understand exactly what you need from nature in order to use it as a healing tool. This model is adapted from a meta-analysis of cancer patients' needs completed by Blaschke, O'Callaghan, and Schofield in 2018, but it's immensely applicable to your trauma healing process, too.

Meaningful Connections

It's very common to feel alone after a traumatic incident. No one was there to help you, and no one can actually comprehend what you're going through. Sometimes you don't even want to be with yourself, as your mind can be a constant loop of flashbacks from that traumatic incident. Being alone is not conducive to healing, and nature can act as a connecting point to yourself, others, and a higher force (side note: whether you're religious or not, being plugged in to some higher power can be helpful and healthy). Nature can also allow you to connect with parts of your past and future that seem lost or impossible to achieve when faced with a traumatic incident. The beauty and peace found in nature open up more doors within us than you might think to be possible.

Furthermore, nature can serve as a sort of attachment figure or a maternal and caring presence in your life. It absolutely acts as a co-therapist when you're working with an eco-therapist, but on its own, it still holds the power to serve as a preliminary attachment figure that can both model healthy relationships with others and introduce those who don't feel safe in relationships to the concept of a positive relationship. You don't have to speak when you're in nature, and you don't have to relate your trauma story to some therapist you don't know or who you feel might not be able to handle the horrors of your past. You just have to show up in whatever state you're in and allow nature to do its work and help you heal.

Distancing Yourself from Your Traumatic Experience

As I said above, sometimes your mind seems like all it wants to do is relive the traumatic experience you survived, and that can drive you crazy. Maybe you're surrounded by remnants of it in the real world, too, whether that be news coverage of the event or loved ones constantly asking you how you're doing. It's completely understandable to just want to GET AWAY, and nature can be that escape. Aside from literally removing yourself from everyday life by spending time in nature, dedicating time to appreciating the outdoors can take your focus off of and give you a welcome reprieve from what's going on surrounding your traumatic event.

Pulling Meaning Out of Your Current Situation

Many trauma survivors have asked themselves over and over again some variation of this question: "Why did this happen to me?" While you will likely never know the answer to that question – and often there *is* no good answer to that question – nature can open self-reflective pathways that can allow you to pull meaning from your healing journey. This may seem too much like "just look on the bright side!" for you, but when you're immersing yourself in all the environments and relationships that exist in nature, you can open yourself to creating relationships, theories, and understandings about your own life and situation. Seeing the complexity, harmony, and interconnectedness of nature can allow you to see that in your own life, too.

Finding Comfort and Safety

A traumatic event, at its core, is a violation of your sense of comfort and personal safety. When that's stripped away from you by a force outside of your control, it can feel nearly impossible to get it back, something that can feel akin to walking through a mall wearing not a stitch of clothing. When you combine the accessibility of nature with any personal value that you place on it, nature can be your cloak of comfort and safety. Furthermore, when you start to realize the protective measures that nature provides its inhabitants – for example, wildlife use trees as shelter from storms – that sense of safety and comfort can transfer to you.

Seeking Physical Nurturing

Though we're discussing healing from psychological trauma as opposed to physical trauma, like a broken leg, healing from anything means caring for all aspects of yourself. Nature offers opportunities for sensory stimulation – watching a sunset, hearing a waterfall, smelling a flower, touching the bark of a tree, or tasting fresh fruit – and physical activity – hiking, climbing, yoga, and many more than I could possibly list here. By combining the psychological benefits and opportunities of nature with the physical ones, spending time in nature can turn into a full-body and full-self healing and nurturing experience.

Ecotherapy

Ecotherapy is the practice of incorporating nature into the therapeutic process. As I discussed earlier in the book, having a mental health professional on your side when healing is not only helpful, but protective of your safety. If you've experienced the healing benefits of nature in your personal life and want to pursue a method of healing that includes nature, consider working with an ecotherapist. You'll get the benefits of both the skills of a mental health professional and time spent in nature! Amy, the aforementioned ecotherapist, describes the difference between using nature alone for healing and working with an ecotherapist through a landscaping example: "You could go out to the garden store, get your own plants, and plant them, and it would probably work out fine. But if you hired a landscaper who knew about the local plants and how to take care of them, things would be different. It's not that the way you did it before without the landscaper wouldn't work; it's just that you get these little, subtle things that you'll learn that can be really helpful." Ecotherapists are great at helping you slow down and be mindful, as mindfulness is an integral part of the therapeutic process, and helping you recognize the little signs and symbols that might go unnoticed if you're on your own.

Amy went on to explain the changes that she saw in some of her trauma clients when she took them out in nature. "You could feel that something really important was happening. You could feel that they were more relaxed outdoors than in my office, and so therefore they were able to open up a little more; they didn't have any kind of psychic defense going on." In ecotherapy, nature is essentially a co-therapist, a bridge between the locked-down emotions and energy of your traumatic event and the open and healing discussion with your therapist. Amy told me the story of one of her clients who was telling her about a lake that she was familiar with, and all of a sudden, all these memories and emotions started spilling out of her about how she lost her dad as a child and how she now recognized that she still had grieving to do. The ecotherapist brings a unique role and skillset to the therapeutic process, but nature brings a whole host of abilities and qualities that are incredibly powerful and unable to be replicated by a human in a traditional talk therapy setting.

Contrary to popular belief, ecotherapy or nature-based therapies do not necessarily have to take place in the wilderness. There are many organizations that do take individuals on wilderness expeditions with the purpose of mental health rehabilitation, but for many individuals, access to that type of nature is limited or nonexistent, especially if you live in a very urban area or are of low socioeconomic status. Therefore, ecotherapy can take place in a variety of places, including local parks, yards or courtyards associated with the therapist's office, or even indoors.

Indoor ecotherapy harnesses many of the benefits of nature (though Amy suggests actually spending time outdoors to get the full range of benefits) but accommodates individuals who cannot or who are not comfortable spending time outdoors. For example, late-stage cancer patients might not be able to complete a nature walk, so indoor ecotherapy could be the perfect fit for them. Indoor ecotherapy involves bringing nature indoors and designing an indoor space with as many outdoor elements as possible. This could take the form of potted plants, nature sounds, aromatherapy, a window with a natural view (or opening the window a touch to let in fresh air and hear the birds), bowls of natural sand with sticks and pinecones that you can play with, or photographs of nature. "A lot of the early brain imaging and MRI studies on the physical benefits of nature were done with people looking at images of nature," Amy said. "Having a picture of a forest on your wall isn't going to cure everything, but I think it's just a little bit that helps." Some therapists also utilize poems about nature for guided imagery practices, which is another way of bringing nature into the office.

Beyond just the differences between indoor and outdoor ecotherapy, different ecosystems can have different effects because of the variances in emotions that they evoke. Deserts, for example, generally evoke feelings of openness and spaciousness, whereas forests might evoke feelings of mysteriousness, quietness, or safety. Different landscapes or microecosystems lend themselves to different activities within the therapeutic process. A grove of trees with sweeping branches and soft sunlight could create a safe environment to talk about something that you're ashamed of or embarrassed about, but the top of a mountain might not be the best place for that because of how exposed it is. That being said, the top of the mountain might be a great space to talk about successes, strengths, and where you're going in life. There isn't one ecosystem that's better for healing from trauma than others, as it all depends on what you're discussing and what that particular ecosystem means and represents to you.

Regardless of where your ecotherapy takes place, Amy describes ecotherapy as pretty non-directive. By this, she means that the therapist and the therapeutic process generally follow your lead, similarly to many of the methods discussed in this book. It's also very experiential, generally non-linear, and often less verbal than indoor therapy. "So much of trauma and what happened is encoded in a non-verbal way," Amy explained, "so it can be hard to express in words how you felt about what happened. With nature, it becomes easier because people can talk in metaphors." Furthermore, it's sometimes easier for the therapist to understand exactly how you're feeling when you're able to use a metaphor to describe it. Amy imagines that ecotherapy "looks like two people hiking, maybe stopping to look at a plant, or a bird flies by and we stop to look at that." These sights – the plant, the bird, or something else that stands out – can serve as a metaphor for something happening in your life. For example, one client of Amy's described her life as a boulder she saw that was squished between two other boulders, meaning that she felt anxious, and Amy was immediately able to understand her client's emotions because she could clearly see the position that her boulder was in.

These recognition moments often come at pauses, whether they're natural – like coming upon a creek that needs to be crossed – or requested by the ecotherapist. During these pauses, you're encouraged to notice how you feel, what thoughts or emotions are coming up for you as you look at whatever it is that you're observing, or what part of the scene in front of you draws your attention. Just as with equine-assisted therapy, this can cause you to become aware of significant symbols that link the natural scene in front of you to your own life and story, like the woman who analogized the boulders with her life and her anxiety. For another example, Amy was working with a client who noticed a particular tree when she was able to pick her head up and notice what was going on around her. She wondered if she did that – being unaware of what was happening around her – in her daily life, and if that played a role in her anxiety. In other words, she used the recognition of a cool tree as a metaphor for something that she struggles with in daily life, and this enabled her to understand her inner processes better. "I find slowing down and asking clients to notice what's around them at certain times sometimes brings in some interesting things," Amy said. "Engaging the senses – touch, smell, obviously sight, hearing – can be really interesting to help clients get back in touch with their bodies and their senses. It can lead to some really interesting paths that are surprising, that end up being really helpful insights to whatever they're working on." When you're able to use metaphors and mirroring in a natural and authentic manner, it can help you both open up to the professional that you're speaking to and understand yourself, your trauma, and your tendencies on a deeper and clearer level.

Another incredible benefit of ecotherapy, as opposed to traditional talk therapy, is the accelerated rate at which it can occur. "You'll have a session with a client where you leave feeling like you made so much more progress than you ever would have in weeks or months," Amy explained. She also confirmed that many other ecotherapists have experienced the same phenomenon. "Sometimes people can come into ecotherapy and the entire therapy process is a shorter process." She went on to tell the story of a client who visited her weekly for three months of traditional talk therapy, and the sessions would always come around to her wondering what to do about one particular problem. Amy finally suggested an ecotherapy session, as she knew that this particular client liked being outdoors, and they went hiking. When they reach a junction in the trail, the client looked both ways and told Amy that she knew what she was going to do about her problem. While ecotherapy does not always have this dramatic of an effect, Amy says that it's not uncommon for rapid changes like this to occur.

How to Use Nature to Heal Without an Ecotherapist

As I've discussed at least twice so far, having a mental health professional as part of your healing journey is beneficial and encouraged, but that doesn't mean that you can't reap the benefits of nature outside of an ecotherapy session. Amy even occasionally gives her clients homework, so there's no reason that you can't give yourself some homework and a prescription for time in nature. There's no one way that you should spend time in nature in order to reap the therapeutic benefits; just make sure that you're doing something you love, whether that's hiking, playing a soccer game, or sitting in a rose garden for a little while. Furthermore, you can still observe metaphors in nature and use them as inspiration or self-understanding.

For example, if you recognize that you always feel better when you sit by a particular tree on your family's farm, then, by all means, go sit by that tree when life gets hard.

If you're unsure what calms you and heals you, then it's time to explore different landscape features! Try different parks, try different elevations, try different terrains, and try different ecosystems. See if you gravitate toward one space over another and see what comes up for you at each of those spaces. When you find a space that is healing and therapeutic for you, spend time there with the goal of simply being in nature. While having a goal of summiting the mountain or running ten miles is great and healthy in many settings, simply being in nature relieves some pressure to succeed and allows you to become mindful of your emotions and their links to your trauma. It's similar to the benefits reaped from the non-goal-oriented nature of dance-movement therapy.

When you've identified this place, you can use it as an emergency healing method, if you will. If you have a flashback, a bad day, or high levels of anxiety, you now know that you can return to this particular place to feel calm. It might only last the rest of the day, but it's free, it's not confined to a schedule, it can be used as many times and as frequently as you need, and you know it works because you've put in the experiential research to determine that.

You can also take a page out of the indoor ecotherapy book and spruce up your work and home spaces with natural items to reap some of the benefits of nature, even if you're trapped in a maze of cubicles. Aside from the methods of indoor ecotherapy discussed above, you can take pictures of the specific therapeutic environments that you've identified and place them in your workspace and home or set them as the background for your phone or computer. You can also download free apps or look up YouTube compilations of nature sounds and play those while you work.

With a combination of these methods, you can build yourself a therapeutic plan that's more than just waiting desperately for your next ecotherapy session. You can use the images and sounds during the day to help you stay calm and focused while at work, then visit your calming nature spot after work to re-center yourself and ease some of that anxiety. That daily ritual can help you maintain your healing level or improve it a bit until your weekly ecotherapy session, at which you can make larger breakthroughs and have deeper discussions with your ecotherapist. While finding a combination that works well for you is imperative, this method of stacking healing and relaxation methods on top of each other to sustain yourself while you heal or go through a therapy process is a simple and effective place for you to start.

The best part about nature and the characteristic of it that makes it an excellent "at-home" therapy is that it's incredibly accessible. Going to regular therapy can be quite difficult, both in terms of scheduling and finances. If you work a traditional 9-to-5 job and your therapist is open from 8am to 4pm, you won't be able to make it to a session unless your boss is willing to give you time off work to go during the day. While this could range from uncomfortable to ask about to having zero chance of your boss allowing it, making it to therapy with a full-time job can be hard. Even if you're a stay-at-home parent, you have to find something to do with your kids while you go to therapy – do you hire a sitter, bring them with you, or wait until your partner gets home? If you choose to wait, then you're back in the same boat of being outside of business hours.

From a financial perspective, as unfortunate as it is, therapy is expensive, especially if you don't have insurance or pursue methods that are not covered by insurance. As we discussed in the second chapter, a potential adult outcome of extensive and complex childhood trauma is a lower reported salary or even unemployment. These are the people that need quality therapy the most, yet they are the people for whom most therapy is inaccessible. These individuals, if they even go to therapy at all, end up at low-cost community therapy clinics. While it's great that they found a way to go to therapy, these types of clinics often have the worst quality of care because the therapists there are brand new and just starting out their careers. Everyone has to start somewhere, but it's a double-edged sword because the people who need therapy the most get low-quality care and the new therapists get burnt out because of the fast-paced and demanding environment they're in. This is where nature comes in. While I would still highly suggest that you work with a trained mental health professional, as well, nature is a fantastic way to bring some healing into your life on your own schedule and for next to nothing in terms of cost. Everyone has access to their front porch, or a city park, or a community garden. Everyone can go look at the stars at night, or take a breath of fresh air, or listen to some birds singing. If traditional therapy is not possible for you, start with nature, and take it from there.

Chapter 15:
Flower Essence Therapy

⳼⳼

E veryone's a little familiar with the language of flowers or, at least, you've heard of the fact that different flowers mean different things when given to someone. Flowers, specifically their essences, are actually able to help trauma survivors, as well, through a method of therapy called flower essence therapy. Flower essence therapy harnesses the unique power of nature and combines it with flowers' ability to resonate with the body to create a unique therapeutic experience that isn't as "out-there" as you'd think. Though it's a blooming (pun totally intended) field in the US, it's actually quite popular in other places in the world. For example, many pharmacies in Spain sell flower essences, and flower essence therapy is incorporated into socialized healthcare in Switzerland, standard hospital practice in Brazil, and the healthcare system in Cuba. It just hasn't taken as strong of roots in the US yet, but it's still accessible if it's a method of healing that you'd like to pursue.

The actual flower essences used in the therapy are not the essential oils of the plant, like in aromatherapy. Loey Colebeck, a flower essence therapist, describes the essences as "a water-based medicine that carries the energetic blueprint of a plant." The essence is made by placing the flower on the surface of a bowl of natural spring water and then placing the bowl in the sun under very specific climate conditions for hours. The sun photographs the essence of the flower into the water, and it's the water that's used in flower essence therapy. There's also a boiling method of making flower essences, where the flower would be boiled in water. The plant material is then strained out so that only the water remains – it's actually only water (with a little bit of brandy or cognac as a preservative) in the flower essence bottle you're using!

It's incredibly dilute, as well, so it's odorless (another contrast to aromatherapy and essential oils). The water that comes directly from the bowls or boiling process is placed in a mother stock, and two drops of the mother stock are added to more natural spring water and the alcoholic preservative to make the stock bottles that you'd buy in a store. This, then, can be further diluted into a smaller, dosing bottle, where it's often combined with other types of essences. In these 1oz dosing bottles, it's only two drops from the stock bottle. "If you took it to the laboratory, they'd say 'This is water,'" Loey explained, "but water holds information. It's like the blueprint; it's not the actual house. It's like a blueprint that speaks to the blueprint in the human system." It's not about receiving any of the actual flower juices (for lack of a better word) in flower essence therapy; it's about receiving a copy of the essence

166

that's been transferred to and transported by the natural spring water. While this can be somewhat of an abstract concept, especially when speaking about photographing flower essences into water, rest assured that flower essence therapy is not simply the placebo effect, as proved by Campanini in 1997 – but more on that in the section on how flower essence therapy works.

Not just any flower is used in flower essence therapy, though. Dr. Edward Bach, a surgeon and the founder of flower essence therapy, named 38 flowers as the main ones used in flower essence therapy. He started selecting flowers by watching personality traits and finding the flower that best resonated with it. This gave him twelve, and he added seven "helper" flowers to the mix that would address personality aspects that the first twelve didn't. To complete his set of 38, he used himself as a sort of human test subject and found 19 more flowers that resonated with him. The way that these flowers were chosen was based on personality instead of illnesses. Dr. Bach found that it was more effective to treat the person *instead* of the illness. That's why it's nearly impossible to choose a certain combination of flower essences that would be best for trauma. Flower essence therapy doesn't treat PTSD; it helps with the emotions and personality aspects, and everyone has a unique personality and reacts differently to trauma. That being said, Star of Bethlehem and rock rose are very common in flower essence therapy for trauma survivors. Star of Bethlehem helps rewire the system, and rock rose helps calm down your adrenals and minimize the effect of the flight-fight-freeze response. These could be some of many flower essences in a

167

personalized mixture that your flower essence therapist will make for you, and the other essences will address your personality: how are you dealing with your trauma? How are you running away from your trauma? How are you coping with your trauma? These are the types of personality questions that would help the flower essence therapist determine which flower essences are right for you, and this determination would be made after an in-depth interview with you, just like a treatment plan would be made up after an interview with a traditional therapist.

How Does Flower Essence Therapy Work?

Flower essence therapy works through resonance. It's more conceptual than chemical, but it makes sense and it's been shown to work time and time again. Humans interact with nature on so many levels, from eating plants and animals to experiencing the benefits of nature discussed in the last chapter, so it's not really a stretch to say that we can interact with flowers on a certain level, as well. In nature, there are patterns of resonance and patterns in how things move, grow, consist of, and appear everywhere. "There can be certain patterns in a plant that can have a poetry to them that speaks to states in the human being," Loey explained. "The best and simplest way to talk about it is qi. We're talking about plants that have a specific type of energy that resonate with a specific type of energy in humans." The goal of flower essence therapy is to use this resonance to move things in the body; in the case of trauma, the goal of flower essence therapy would be to use the resonance of flower energy to move the portion of trauma that's stuck in the body.

As I've discussed before with the definition of trauma and with dance-movement therapy, your emotions, reactions, and energy toward and during your traumatic event get stuck in the body. Different disciplines might call this different things – flower essence therapists often call it crystalized energy – but the result is still the same. There's still a part of your mind, body, and soul that's stuck, immobile, and preventing you from healing. To help cope with your trauma and all of its side effects, many people turn to things like indulging, over-working, or something else entirely. This is where flower essence therapy comes in. "Flower essences can work with all of these different survival strategies," Loey said. "As far as actually going in and helping rewire the circuitry and release that crystalized energy, there are flower essences that help make those new connections so that energy can be released." Furthermore, various flower essences can help calm the nervous system, both in general and during triggering events.

Let's stick with that "calming the nervous system" concept in order to give you an example that can help you understand how flower essences work. Just like I talked about in the dance-movement therapy chapter, healing from trauma often requires that you complete the cycle, moving through the trapped stress in your body so that you can release it. Flower essences can help your nervous system handle those releases. "They accompany the person as they make those emotional releases so that they're not so overwhelming," Loey added. Rock rose is one flower essence that helps calm the nervous system and adrenal response, as I said above, so people who receive rock rose essence can take an emotional system that's running on all cylinders, calm it down, and refocus some of that energy to moving through the emotions that are buried in their trauma. In other words, flower essences can make the surface emotions and reactions more manageable so you can devote more time to addressing and moving through your stuck trauma.

Don't believe in the efficacy of flower essence therapy? A study by Campanini in 1997 showed that three to four months of flower essence therapy treatment resulted in an 89% improvement in anxiety, stress, and depression in the study's subjects. An analysis by Dr. Jeffrey Cram of five studies examining the efficacy of flower essence therapy showed a 50-80% decrease in depression symptoms in an average of just three months of therapy. Two case studies by Ross in 2010 showed that flower essence therapy for young individuals with learning challenges and emotional trauma improved their maturity, independence, and ability to focus; decreased their fear, self-centeredness, and anxiety; and helped them relax. Finally, a study by Holthuis in 2018 examined the effects of flower essence therapy on young adults in shelters who had experienced severe trauma in their life and found incredibly positive results. First of all, the individuals who used the Rescue Remedy (see the section about finding flower essences for your personal use at the end of this chapter) during crisis or triggers found that it helped them calm down. Secondly, of the individuals who received a personalized flower essence blend and used it for a series of months, 90% reported an improvement in their general well-being and 50% said that the flower essences met or exceeded their expectations. Some of the testimonials in the study from the individuals who used the flower essence blends specify improvements such as an increased ability to set boundaries, not "feeling like a piece of trash anymore", and an improvement in the individuals' abilities to stay calm during stressful situations.

The best part of all of these studies that I just shared? The 1997 Campanini study examined the effects of skepticism on flower essence therapy, and it had absolutely no effect. This means that flower essence therapy is not a placebo, something that you believe works and therefore you see improvements in your symptoms. No, flower essence therapy works in and of itself, no matter what you might think of it.

What Happens During Flower Essence Therapy?

When you first attend flower essence therapy, plan on being there for about an hour and a half. This first session is all about the flower essence therapist finding out where you're at right now and how you've approached your healing so far. If you're at the beginning of your healing journey and your emotions are still running on high, the flower essence therapist might address those emotions with a few remedies before diving into the meat of your trauma. Your therapist will take the information he or she receives from you (both on health history forms and through discussion of where you're at) and make a personalized remedy of flower essences that you'll work with at home for a period of weeks. This usually occurs through ingestion of the essences, but occasionally you'll use them topically for localized symptoms. Flower essence therapy is rarely a one-and-done method; it can take multiple applications of the flower essences to result in a positive effect, a process Loey described as "a slow drip."

The in-office, face-to-face portion of flower essence therapy is less frequent than most other therapies, which can make this method appealing to those who don't want to or are unable to attend in-person sessions frequently. Follow-up sessions occur every two to three weeks in flower essence therapy. The reason for this is that you have additional prescribed support at home through the flower essences. The in-office portion of flower essence therapy often looks like talk therapy with other mind-body approaches thrown in, such as body awareness exercises and meditation. In between sessions, you'll be fortifying yourself in your healing journey through homework activities, such as journaling, going on walks, or changing your diet around.

All About Flower Essence Therapists

Flower essence therapy is, unfortunately, not as regulated as other forms of therapy and other types of therapists. A background, degree, or certification is not required to practice flower essence therapy and, even further, there is no one certifying body or set of educational requirements for practicing flower essence therapy. If you're looking to work with a flower essence therapist, though, there are some ways to make sure that you're working with a good one. First of all, make sure that you read the client bill of rights carefully. The client bill of rights is a document that describes what your rights as a client are and what sort of training the practitioner has gone through. Secondly, simply ask the practitioner about their training and educational background. Loey runs an introductory course that's one year long and contains 100 hours of training, but you're not considered a competent flower essence therapist after just that. Therefore, if the therapist you're considering says something along the lines of "I've trained for 100 hours" or "I've done a year of training", then they probably don't have the expertise that you're looking for. If they say that they've done more training – or, even better, say that they've been mentored by an experienced flower essence therapist – then I'd still consider them in the running.

My personal recommendation to ensure that you get the best care possible would be to start with the mental health side and add on the flower essence therapy, just like with finding a trauma-sensitive yoga instructor. If you look for mental health professionals who practice flower essence therapy instead of looking for flower essence therapists (and hoping that their two-day mental health first aid course is sufficient), you're more likely to find someone qualified to both practice flower essence therapy and to care for your psychological needs through the healing process. Any time that you're releasing trauma, you need to be in an environment with someone who knows how to control the release and allow it to happen in a safe manner – I'm pretty sure I've said a variation of this in every chapter so far, so you know it's important! Having someone there to hold the space for you and help you through it is critical, so narrow your search to mental health professionals and find a flower essence therapist in that pool.

Having the flower essence therapy piece is equally important, though, because of their ability to accurately create a mixture of flower essences that will work for you. "If you don't know anything about the medicine [of flower essences] and you're walking into the store and looking at a little two-sentence description and think, 'Oh, that sounds about right!' and you try that, it's hit or miss, and it's usually miss," Loey said. "Would you walk into a pharmacy and walk behind the counter and read a two-sentence description of a pill and think, 'Oh, that sounds about right,' and take it?" – hopefully not – "We're talking about medicine that's powerful and works when it's chosen correctly, so working with someone who has training and knows what they're doing makes all the difference." Just because flower essences don't come in little pills from a pharmaceutical company doesn't mean that they're not powerful and effective, so the person you choose to work with needs to be skilled in both mental healthcare and flower essences.

Luckily, though, nothing will happen if you take the wrong one – and I mean literally nothing. You will feel no benefit from the wrong flower essence, and you won't feel any negative side effects, save for the fact that your belief in flower essence therapy might be dashed. In fact, Loey believes that if you feel a "negative" side effect, you're probably taking the right one. "It's catalyzing some sort of crisis of what needs to come out. If you take a remedy and, all of a sudden, you're feeling really sad, like you just need to cry and cry, it's probably the right remedy." Don't worry, though. These negative-but-actually-positive side effects are much gentler than the negative side effects of traditional pharmaceutical medicines, and even much gentler than homeopathy.

Where to Find Flower Essences for Personal Use

The main brand of flower essences is Bach Flower Remedies, named after the founder of flower essence therapy. The Bach Remedies are distributed through Directly From Nature, and you can view all of their products at www.directlyfromnature.com/?Click=69584. I highly recommend working with a flower essence therapist to determine which flower essences are right for you, but there's a collection of essences called Rescue Remedies that are perfect for personal purchase and use without a flower essence therapist. There are various forms of Rescue Remedies, like drops or sprays, but they all are a mixture of the same five flower essences, one of which is Star of Bethlehem. The Rescue Remedies are designed for immediate relief of stress, panic, terror, and dissociation, so they're great to have on-hand for daily stresses or triggers. A study by Halberstein and colleagues in 2007 actually tested the effects of the Rescue Remedies by having the participants take four drops of the remedy five times throughout the course of the experiment. They found that taking Rescue Remedies for high levels of anxiety – such as during triggers or immediately upon experiencing a trauma – significantly decreased the level of anxiety as opposed to a placebo. In other words, Rescue Remedies work for acute situations! Not to end this chapter on a warning, but it's important to note that Rescue Remedies won't completely help you heal from trauma. They are great for acute situations and high-stress scenarios, but they don't get at the underlying emotions or stored trauma in your body. You need a flower essence therapist and a personalized essence combination for that.

Chapter 16:
Which Therapy is Right for Me?

⚮

Unfortunately (but really fortunately), this is a very individual decision. The information that I gave you about the various therapeutic methods, as well as my personal experiences with them, should give you some guidance as far as a good place to start, but you need to pick the therapeutic method that feels the best to you. For example, you may feel like equine-assisted therapy would be the best fit for you, but when you arrive on an equine-assisted therapy facility, you realize that it doesn't feel "right". "Not right" could mean unsafe, uncomfortable, or whatever that means to you, but don't pigeonhole yourself into one therapeutic method if you find that it isn't the right fit for you.

Beyond that, each therapist has their own way of doing things, even within a therapeutic method. If you find that the therapist you're working with doesn't feel right but believe that the method is a good fit for you, I highly encourage you to find a new therapist. Don't feel like you have to stay with someone once you start with them; your healing is the most important part of the equation, so finding someone that you trust and that you work well with is critical.

That being said, I'll try to give you some suggestions of which therapy might be best for you by summarizing the key traits of the methods I've discussed. I am not qualified to give you medical advice as far as which therapy is best for you and, in reality, it's important for you to have control over your choices, including which therapy method you pursue. Therefore, take the following as a suggestion, not a direction, and feel free to experiment if the first therapeutic method you try isn't right for you.

If you like hanging out with animals...

For many of us, we understand the calming nature that animals bring into our lives, whether that's from having pets of our own or interacting with animals on a regular basis. If you believe that animals have a positive psychological or spiritual effect on your life – or simply enjoy hanging out with animals – then consider trying canine-assisted therapy, equine-assisted therapy, or dolphin-assisted craniosacral therapy.

If you like being outside...

As with animals, I'm sure there are loads of individuals – maybe you! – who believe in the healing power of nature. Maybe you've experienced it for yourself, or maybe you find a little bit of peace from the nature photograph that hangs on your living room wall. If that's the case, perhaps nature-based therapies or ecotherapy would be a good fit for you. I would also consider equine-assisted therapy if you like being out-doors. It's a different setting – pastures, as opposed to parks or wilderness – but it's outside with sunshine and fresh air all the same.

If you like moving...

If being still is uncomfortable and you like moving when you're talking or physical activity in general, there are a few suggestions I have. First, as the name implies, dance-movement therapy might be a good fit for you. As I described in its chapter, it's not dance as much as freedom of movement, but it's movement nonetheless. Another suggestion is the Epona model of equine-assisted therapy. This incorporates therapeutic riding and movement on horseback. My final sug-gestion would be trauma-sensitive yoga. As with dance-move-ment therapy, it's not yoga as much as freedom of choice in which movements you participate in, but it does allow for more movement than, say, EMDR.

If you like using symbols to explain your life...

If you like talking in metaphors and using symbols to

explain parts of your life, then ecotherapy or the EAGALA model of equine-assisted therapy might be a good fit for you. Both of these therapies use elements of your surroundings (meaning horses or parts of the landscape) as symbols and metaphors, which can make communicating about your emotions and your trauma easier.

If releasing the physical part of trauma is most important to you...

All of the therapeutic methods discussed address the physical *and* emotional parts of trauma in some form. In fact, one of the keys of natural and integrative methods of healing from trauma is the incorporation of releasing the trauma that's stored in the body. During my research about the various therapeutic methods, though, there were two therapies that had the theme of "releasing the trauma that's stored in the body" coming up more frequently than in other therapies: dance-movement therapy and craniosacral therapy. If relieving yourself of the physical weight of trauma is important to you, then it might be worthwhile starting with one of those two methods. Unfortunately, craniosacral therapy is not usually covered by insurance (though it can be financed through a Health Savings Account), so if finances are a large part of your decision process, then it might be worthwhile trying another method first. That being said, I'm all for investing in yourself, and there's really no better investment you could make than ridding your body of trauma.

If reshaping mental pathways is important to you...

Obviously, the ideal trauma healing program would include healing both the somatic part of trauma and the emotional part of trauma, but some methods directly address one more prominently than the other. EMDR is the therapy that most directly addresses the mental pathways surrounding your memory of your trauma and your emotions about yourself. Mindfulness and meditation practices are also great at addressing the mental aspect of trauma, though they more help you control your mind during triggering events or stressful situations as opposed to recoding the memories of your trauma. Both are great methods to pursue, though, if healing the mental part of your trauma is a priority to you.

If you like very fluid and client-directed methods of therapy...

Some therapies, such as EMDR, are very structured. There's an eight-step process to conducting EMDR, and there's very little say that you have in terms of changing the process. Sure, you can decline EMDR or push it back toward a later date, but there's an inherent structure to the therapy. If you're looking for something with less structure and that gives you a lot of control over what happens during the session, consider trauma-sensitive yoga, EAGALA equine-assisted therapy, dance-movement therapy, or ecotherapy. All of these therapies are heavily client-directed and allow you to do what feels right to you and your body.

If you don't like spending as much time in the therapist's office...

Because of that fact that you have flower essences to work with at home, flower essence therapy sessions in the therapist's office are much less frequent than other forms of therapy. Though this is a general guideline, your therapist and you will decide on a frequency of visits, and that might not be every week. Also, flower essence therapy, like craniosacral therapy, is not covered by insurance (except for in the countries mentioned in the flower essence therapy chapter), so keep that in mind when considering using flower essence therapy in your healing journey. If it's more the office that you don't like being in – as opposed to the frequency of seeing your therapist – then consider the methods that take place outdoors, like equine-assisted therapy or ecotherapy.

What Did I Do?

Well...none of the above, and I'd say that's my greatest regret in my healing process. Personally, I cried a lot. I spent a lot of time alone, reflecting, but I also surrounded myself with a great support system that I could talk to, rant to, and cry with (Kayla, Sophia, Liz, Lynn, Brian – thank you for the parts you played in my story). I dug myself up, handhold by handhold, and I fought, every single day.

I also wrote. I remember being at summer camp at the start of the decline of my mental health, watching a sunset over

a beautiful rock forest that we had spent all day climbing.
Here's what I wrote:

Hard rock edges, jagged walls
A steep ascent, a lonely haul
Alone in a cavern, wasting away
Stuck in myself, stuck day after day

I only see the thing I place in front of me
The mirror that speaks back to me and tells me what to see
I cannot see beyond that wall to see what is inside
The lonely cav'rn a wall of mirrors; I curl up and I hide

All the mirrors beat me down
I've nothing left; on the ground
I have some days where hope's light shines in
I claw myself up to where I begin

The light reflects the mirror's image back into my eyes
The image that I'm shown in seared into my mind
My fingers sweat and start to slip; I fall back down again
Fall back down the lonely cliff, no purchase left to gain

Hiding once again from the world I do not know
Walls go up, masks go on - nothing left to show
Imprisoned in my cavern, where I am all alone
Walls of mirrors beat me down with images of stone

I smirk, looking back at this poem, because sunsets are now

the most beautiful parts of my day. I love watching them light up the sky every single night. It brings me peace and it brings me serenity; it reminds me that even though something ends in flames, it can still be beautiful. Anyway, words have always been powerful for me, whether that's quotes, poetry, or writing. Knowing that about myself, I wrote another poem that described all the beautiful things I wanted in my life:

From tops of snowcapped mountains to ocean waves below
The stream of life bestows its breath into my very soul
I see the world for what it is: a beautied reverie
And understand that time will pass in methods up to me

I feel the rapid passion that comes and takes me far
That carries me through grand adventures sitting on a star
I feel the calming breeze that makes me stop and rest
And realize that the universe inhabits a mere breath

I always find beside me the smiles of those I love
And words of those who have me passed rest on the wings of doves
Hands turn into hearts and hearts turn into homes
And souls become divided 'tween the places I have roamed

A picture can preserve a moment for a year or two
But when enclosed in memory, the feelings remain new
My bank of memories is full yet still has room for more
I've kept on adding times of joy and love into my store

Spine stood straight and head held high I take my every step

Climb one more rung of life's long ladder 'til I reach the tip
I give the gift of precious love to everyone I crave
So that I fill my life with time and moments I can save

This poem is all about choice, having loved ones nearby, and appreciating the natural beauty of the world – a far cry from jagged rocks and being trapped in caverns. I memorized this second poem, and when life would start to get out of control, when I'd start to breakdown, or when I'd begin to panic, I would step away, find a quiet place, and whisper this poem to myself. It reminded me that I had good things worth living for and that I was the designer of my future, not my trauma and relatively non-existent self-esteem.

Though I don't regret writing and taking time for myself, I wish I would have included formal therapy in my healing process. I don't think I ever would have been successful doing CBT or talk therapy, but I wish I knew about some of the methods that I've taught you about here. I wish I knew that spending time making snow angels in a field of horses was therapy. I wish I knew that sitting by a river and talking about how life feels like getting squished by two boulders was therapy. I wish I knew that I had options, that I had choices, and that there were professionals who would support me in them, instead of forcing me to talk about or do something that I wasn't comfortable with. I do believe that I've healed, but I also feel like I would have healed faster and deeper if I included a formal therapy method in my journey. I'm praying that you don't have the same regrets that I do.

Chapter 17:
What Happens After Healing?

ᘓ᙭᙭ᘒ

C ongratulations! You've taken some really hard steps, moved through your recovery process, and...what now? While any combination of confusion, fear, and freedom might be going through your head, there's probably a common thread of "what the heck do I do now?" You've spent a significant amount of time and brain energy living with and healing from a trauma, and it's been the primary focus of your life for a long time. You might feel like you've dedicated enough of your life to this traumatic incident and that it's time to move on from it completely, but unfortunately – or rather, fortunately – that's not the case.

You can heal, but you can't get rid of your trauma.

Wait... what? I'm seriously sitting here, at the end of this book about how to heal from trauma, saying that you can't completely remove that traumatic incident from your life? Yes, and no. I and many of the professionals that I spoke to agree that it's almost impossible to imagine someone completely healing from trauma to the point where they never think about it or never experience a trigger, no matter how minor. For example, there will still be days where I'll see my friend pop up on social media, or his mom will comment on one of my posts, or I'll see someone who looks like him walking down the street. Those days definitely evoke a healthy dose of nostalgia and a little doubt, as well. Is he happy? Did I make a positive impact in his life by calling the cops all those years ago? Does he still love me like I love him, or does he still hate me for betraying his trust? These are questions that I haven't been able to answer in the weeks, months, and years since that night, and they're not questions that I think I'll ever answer. They still come up occasionally in my life, but whether that says that I still have some grieving to do or that this is how I'm going to live from here on out, I'm not sure.

I tend to lean toward the latter, though, that this present reality of occasionally reminiscing on our time spent together and wondering about the impact I made is the culmination of my healing journey. This is because a commonly agreed upon definition of "healed from trauma" is getting to the point where the trauma doesn't control your life. "I do think that, with work and with treatment, on your own or with a therapist, I do think – actually, I know – that any of us can get to a place where it's not controlling our lives anymore, and we can get to a place where it's just kind of in the background," Amy, the ecotherapist, says. "Maybe there's always going to be a little thing where we sort of are reminded of it, but it doesn't completely have to overtake our lives anymore. We can just go about our lives basically not thinking about it." For me, I can go through 99% of my days without crying over our interactions. I don't have a breakdown every time I see someone who looks like him. I am not constantly plagued by thoughts and memories of what happened between us. My trauma does not control my life anymore, and I would consider having *your* trauma not controlling your life anymore a fantastic end goal for you to set for yourself.

I would even go so far as to say that having your trauma not control your life anymore is a better goal to set than having your trauma completely eradicated from your life. Suffering and trauma have been parts of the human existence since our beginnings, and while I would never wish a traumatic event on anyone, there are some positives that can come out of such a horrendous event, namely empathy, compassion, and strength.

Every moment of your life acts like a puzzle piece. Every single piece of food you put in your mouth contributes to the puzzle that is your body and your physical health. Every single song lyric and tidbit of knowledge that you've learned contribute to your brain and your intellect. Similarly, every single situation you've experienced contributes to the puzzle that is your soul. Positive or negative, these experiences have made you who you are, and part of this healing process is being proud of yourself for the complex, flawed, and utterly beautiful person that you are and learning to own the pieces that might not be your favorite. Yes, that means you need to own and love your trauma. Your trauma doesn't define you anymore, and you're able to have a new and more positive relationship with it.

As I said at the beginning of the book, no person reacts to a traumatic incident the same way and no person heals the same way. Each step that you've taken on this journey – from the incident itself to the completion of your healing process – has given you insight into yourself and into the world that no one else has. This is not a curse, a scar, or a debilitation that you have to carry with you for the rest of your life. As Sally from Acres for Life put it, "it is your strength, and it can become your gift." This is your opportunity to take something horrible that has happened to you, stitch it into the fabric of your soul, and use it to light the lives of those around you. You don't have to take up a career in advocacy or dedicate all of your time to volunteering at a battered women's shelter; simply conquering and accepting your trauma is enough of a light to impact the people around you. When you're able to accept and share your brokenness and your light, you will be able to relate to people on a much deeper level, a level that can positively impact the both of you.

Now, this can get a little tricky. Am I saying that you have a *right* to use your trauma to inspire and help others? Absolutely. Am I saying that you have a *responsibility* to use your trauma to inspire and help others? No, but…when you've overcome something so personally harmful as a traumatic incident, you will develop a strength that will exude from you, whether you're wanting it to or not. Even if you don't share your story with someone – even if you don't say a word – being a person of strength in the life of your friends and family members is inspiration and help in itself. Therefore, if you're the type of person who wants to get on with your life after a traumatic incident, you're completely able to. You'll just be impacting the lives of others quietly and subconsciously, which is just as powerful as spoken, public advocacy and service.

Just as a traumatic incident impacts the puzzle that is your soul, it can also have a large impact on your values and life goals. Some things might not seem as important after you've been through a traumatic event, whereas others will seem so critically important that you're smacking yourself for not paying more attention to them earlier in your life. Don't beat yourself up over this; growth is a part of healing and a part of life, and sometimes growth means change. That being said, it's important to take some time to reassess your life and where you're going.

Figure out what you want to do with your life now that you've healed from your trauma.

Any major life change – whether that be positive, like a marriage, or negative, like a trauma – can cause what you thought you knew about your life to change. Knowing how to accept that change and how to move with it is the most important part. You aren't a quitter or a failure because what was important to you doesn't seem as critical anymore. You're not lost because you have the whole world in front of you and you don't know what to do with it.

At this point, the most important thing is designing a life that's authentic. You are no longer living trapped under your trauma, so don't you decide to start living for someone else or according to what someone else thinks you should do. As I like to say, should-hoods are shit-hoods. In other words, don't do something because someone says you should do it; do it because it aligns with your values and brings you closer to your goals. The world is full of possibilities, and your job is to decide which of them aligns with the self you want to be and pursue them.

My recommendation is to spend some time evaluating what happiness, success, and fulfillment look like to you, then deciding how to pursue a life that embodies your definition of those characteristics. Again, don't listen to what your family, friends, or society says about what happiness, success, and fulfillment should look like. Just like your trauma journey is unique, your definition of those characteristics is unique.

If you're still unsure, pick a few things, try them out, and see how they feel. If you feel like you've come home when you're doing those activities or hanging out with those people, then you're headed in the right direction. If you feel uncomfortable or inauthentic, then it's probably time to try something else. Remember, your new goals in life are to live authentically and to have some fun while doing it. You've been thrown to the bottom of a ravine then climbed up, step by step. You deserve a life filled with happiness, success, and fulfillment. You've conquered the mountain, and now it's time to reap the benefits and opportunities of your success. I wish you the best of luck in your new future.

Chapter 18:
How to Help Someone Healing from Trauma

✿✿✿

I   f you're paying particular note to this chapter, my heart hurts for you. Having someone you love, whether that's a friend or family member, experience a trauma is painful for you, as well, but I applaud you for exploring the best ways to help them. Take some time to absorb the concepts in this chapter and try not to let your enthusiasm about helping them get in the way of your relationship. How you handle this situation could make or break your relationship with the survivor – they could push you away completely, or you could become an incredibly important pillar of support for them during this indescribably difficult time.

Things NOT to Say

When someone you love is going through something traumatic, the first thing you want to do is be there for them, and while that's fantastic, certain things you say can do more harm than good. While you may be well-intentioned, it often doesn't sit right with the survivor and can often come across as insincere or ignorant. Avoid saying these, and instead opt for the "best things to say" that I'll cover next.

"I know what you're going through."

Um… no you don't! Unless you went through the exact – and I mean *exact* – same trauma and have the same physiological and psychological makeup as your friend or family member, you don't know what they're going through. Saying this can seem like you're minimizing the effect of the trauma: "Oh, it's no big deal, I went through the same thing!" For the survivor, this trauma is incredibly important and incredibly hurtful, and, even more importantly, it's *theirs*. While they may not want it to be this way, they own their experiences and their emotions. Don't take that away from them.

"I'm so sorry for you."

When you tell someone healing from a trauma that you're sorry for them, you're labeling them as a victim and someone requiring sympathy. They are stronger than imaginable for surviving a trauma and coming out the other side. Furthermore, law enforcement and medical professionals may already be labeling them as a victim, and they may be labeling themselves as one, too. Victims are traditionally weak, helpless, and in need of saving – not a pretty or productive mindset to have, and potentially quite embarrassing, too. Don't add to that label by indirectly calling them a victim.

It's so common to tell someone that you're sorry for something happening to them. It's kind of the thing we all say when we want to express sympathy but don't know what else to say. Because of this, "I'm sorry"s can be devalued. I'm of the opinion that you should only apologize when you did something that caused another person harm and when you have the intention to change your actions to prevent it from happening again. But what should you say instead?

My second-favorite alternative is "my heart hurts for you." As I said at the beginning of this chapter, having someone you love go through a trauma can hurt you, as well, and that hurt is as legitimate as the trauma your loved one experienced. Saying something like this lets the trauma survivor know that you're invested in their healing and that they have someone on their side.

My favorite alternative to "I'm so sorry for you" is "I hear you and I'm here for you." This line is so powerful, both in trauma healing and in everyday life. By saying this, you're letting the trauma survivor know that everything they're sharing – their story and their feelings – are heard and received by you and that you're going to be their cheerleader and their support system as they move through the healing process.

It's important to note that, because of how common apologizing is, it'll take some time to swap out the apology for one of the suggested phrases above. It's automatic to apologize, so it could take a lot of conscious thought and maybe a few pauses to consider your words before you stop having the urge to apologize for something you didn't do.

"It could be worse!"

How is this helpful? If anyone out there thinks this is a helpful thing to say to someone, please get in touch with me, because I'd love to have a discussion with you about this. Similarly to telling someone that you know what they're going through, telling them that it could be worse tells them that their emotions and reactions are over-the-top and unwarranted. Every individual responds to trauma differently, and every response is absolutely okay. It is utterly useless to compare the severity of trauma. A favorite saying of mine goes something like this: "The person who drowned in one foot of water and the person who drowned in 20 feet of water are both dead." Any trauma survivor is hurting, struggling, and trying to heal – it doesn't matter whose trauma was "worse".

"It'll be okay."

It might not, or it might not for a while, and that's perfectly okay. Saying this to someone does one of two things (or perhaps both). First of all, it places some imaginary timeline on their healing. Some people recover from a traumatic incident in a week, and some people take 20 years. Every individual needs to work through the healing process at their own pace, and if they're not "okay" for 20 years – that's okay, too. Secondly, telling a survivor this implies that everything goes back to normal after they heal. Sometimes it doesn't. A lot of times it doesn't. Going through something so deep and emotional can change a person, and the person isn't always the same at the other end of it. This is "okay", too, but it's a new version of "okay" that might take some getting used to. Allow them to feel their pain for as long as they need.

A friend of mine who lost her father when she was seven years old told me that this was one of the least helpful things that her friends and family members said to her during the time immediately following her loss. While she was thankful for their support and felt that they played a key role in her healing process, hearing this from them felt like they were invalidating or glossing over her feelings and not giving her the time she needed to grieve. She knew it would be okay eventually, but it wasn't okay *right then*, and she needed to know that it was okay to not be okay. If your friend or family member has been through a traumatic event, keep this friend of mine in mind, as you don't want your friend or family member to experience the same emotions from your attempt to help. Instead, love them, accept them, and support them, but most importantly, allow them to heal at their own rate.

"They didn't mean to hurt you!"

This is probably the most irrelevant thing that you could say to someone healing from a trauma, and I don't mean to be harsh by saying that. I don't care if someone meant to give someone 1,000 pounds of gold but accidentally dropped it on their head – the person is still hurt. The same thing applies to trauma. The focus of the healing journey should not be the intention of the person who caused the trauma but on the reaction of the person who experienced the trauma. There's really no other way to phrase this: it doesn't matter what the person who caused the trauma intended or whether they're a "good person" or not; the person who experienced the trauma is deeply hurt, and you, as the person helping them through the trauma, would be smart to remember that distinction.

"Get over it."

I'm hoping that none of you out there would think that this is a good thing to say to someone, but sadly, many people have experienced this reaction from someone that they're close with. This not only deeply harms the healing journey that the trauma survivor is going through, but it puts up a giant brick wall between you and the survivor. By telling them this, you're telling them that their feelings are too dramatic and that they're taking too long to deal with what happened to them. As I've said before, each healing journey is unique, and you have no way to know how far along someone is or how hard they've fought to get to where they are without being them – and you're not.

"Come on, you should really talk about it!"

Everyone processes their trauma at their own rate, and having you sitting there bugging them to talk about it could force them to speak when they're not ready or push you away from them. A key point in trauma healing is to go at the survivor's pace, whether you're the therapist or a friend or family member just trying to help. Pushing them to take a step before they're ready could be anywhere from impossible to destructive.

When you're reacting in this way and getting all upset because someone won't tell you about their trauma, you need to take a serious look at yourself and ask if you're wanting to help them because you want them to get better or you're wanting to "help them" to satisfy your own curiosity. If it's the latter, it is possible to change and become a safe support system for your friend or family member, but don't make them question what your motives are when you're trying to help them.

"You should do/try _____."

As I'll discuss in the next section, your best role as a friend or family member is to be there and support them – not give them advice on how to heal. If you don't have training as a psychological or psychiatric professional, then you are not qualified to give them advice. Even if you've been through a trauma healing process yourself, there's no guarantee that what worked for you will help them, and you run the risk of harming their healing process if you tell them what to do without having the proper professional training and understanding of their unique situation. If you are someone who has professional training in the field, I would still not recommend giving them advice; rather, direct them to one of your colleagues or suggest a method of therapy that they should pursue.

Things TO Say – or Rather, Do

All right – finally the part that tells you how to help someone going through a trauma. Just as there are a lot of things that you could say that would make a negative impact on someone's healing journey, there are a few key things that you could say – or rather, do – to help them. In fact, it's not as much about the words that you tell someone as how you show them that you're a support system. You don't need to advertise the fact that you're there to help; you just need to be there.

First things first – get yourself sorted out before trying to help someone else.

In order to be a good support system for someone, you need to have yourself sorted out and you need to have your motives in line. Are you trying to help your friend or family member because you love and care about them or because you have an intense curiosity to find out what happened to them (hint: they don't have to tell you)? If it's the former, then you're already in the right headspace, and these next pages can really help you understand how to be a good support system for someone. If it's the latter, then you need to put some work into yourself first. "If you're distressed, if you're activated, if you're living in fear and anxiety and worry, that's not going to help anybody," Hilary explained. "Figure out a way to deal with not knowing. Know that you're not going to know until your loved one wants you to know, and there's a very real possibility that they may never want you to know."

Don't worry, though. If you're struggling to manage your own emotions, both in life and in regards to your friend or family member's trauma, you can turn that around so that you're a positive support system for them. They might invite you to partake in a therapy session with them, and definitely take them up on that offer if it comes around (though don't push them to invite you). They might also come to you with some homework from their therapist that works on strengthening your relationship and your ability to be a support system; take that homework seriously, as it may be the bridge from where you are to being the support system you want to be. If neither of those things happen, then pay close attention to this chapter and seek independent help for managing your emotions. Having someone you love go through a trauma can be traumatizing for you, as well, so there's no shame in talking to a professional about your own thoughts and feelings surrounding the event.

Validate their emotions.

Trauma and its healing processes are confusing and emotional times. Your friend or family member is probably unearthing emotions and memories that are painful to experience, and they often will feel out of control of their thoughts and feelings. If you are able to validate their emotions and let them know that they have the right and the freedom to feel whatever they feel, that can take a load off of their shoulders. During the healing process, energy should not be devoted to feeling insecure or ridiculous about their emotions; having that validation from someone close to them on a personal level can be very positively impactful.

Treat them as normally as possible.

This holds true for a lot of mental health disorders, but it's important to note for trauma survivors, as well. Someone who is healing from a trauma is not broken, nor are they about to break. They don't need to be treated any differently in terms of general social interaction. They don't need to be protected or handled with kid gloves. They are still your friend or family member who you love deeply and who has a prominent spot in your life. Continue to invite them out to social events. Continue your Sunday morning coffee date. Continue complaining about your annoying relationship. Whatever you normally do with that person, continue to do so. This will enable your friend or family member to retain some normalcy in their life during a time that is very, very painfully abnormal.

Hold space for them.

If you're only able to do one thing for your friend or family member, then hold the space for them. What does this mean? Heather Plett, a coach who specializes in holding spaces for people as they undergo personal development journeys, defines holding the space as being "willing to walk alongside another person in whatever journey they're on without judging them, making them feel inadequate, trying to fix them, or trying to impact the outcome. When we hold space for other people, we open our hearts, offer unconditional support, and let go of judgement and control." A perfect example of this was told to me by Sally of Acres for Life. She was playing a game of hide-and-seek with a group of young clients, and she and one girl decided to hide in the dumpster. It was smelly, dark, and very, very gross, and yet the word that Sally used to describe that moment was that is was a "privilege" to be there with that girl.

The mind of someone going through trauma can be just like that dumpster – gross, dark, and not a pleasant place to be. Unfortunately, they can't just hop out of the dumpster whenever they want, and you, as someone wanting to help someone on their healing journey, need to sit in that dumpster. You might want to get out before them and you might not even want to get in there at all, but being willing to sit with someone in their dark place for as long as they need and simply *be* there with them is the best thing that you can do for them.

Heather describes eight steps to holding the space successfully for people, and for those readers who want a bit more instruction, here are those steps:

1. Trust your own intuition and give the trauma survivor permission to trust theirs. There is no guidebook for holding space for someone, just as there's no universal step-by-step process for healing from trauma. Trusting your relationship with the survivor and somewhat going with the flow will help you be successful in holding the space for them.

2. Don't overwhelm your friend or family member with information. While you may feel like handing them a million pamphlets about various therapeutic methods and shoving this book in their face, try to refrain. Their mind is already in overwhelm, and there's no need to add to it or force them into a space where they're not ready to be. Instead, try something like leaving this book on the coffee table when they come over, and if they show interest, offer to let them borrow it for the weekend.

3. Allow the survivor to keep their autonomy. Man, this one can be really hard to do, and I speak from personal experience when I say this. Just as I spoke about treating your friend or family member as normally as possible, it's important to allow them to

make their own decisions (unless it's something life-threatening like suicide or dangerous addictions that require an intervention). This gives them power and control – something they feel they lack because of their trauma – instead of making them feel useless and incompetent.

4. Their failure is not your failure. In other words, keep your ego out of it. If it takes them longer to heal than you would have liked them to, that does not mean that you are a bad friend or that you held the space for them improperly. If your intervention doesn't go as well as you planned, it's not a failing on your part. Their journey is their journey; it is not a reflection on your ability to love them.

5. Create a safe space without judgement or shame. In life and in trauma healing, failure and setbacks are inevitable. We all have those people in our lives that we're afraid to tell that we've failed, and our relationships with them are probably not too good beneath the surface. Don't be that person! Create a safe space for your friend or family member to fail by removing judgement or shame from the equation.

6. Offer them help in a way that doesn't make them feel incompetent. This can be a bit tricky, especially in the psychological world and when the person you're holding the space for is a friend or family member. Mental health professionals do this by guiding their sessions, but you, as a friend or family member of the survivor, can offer to help in other ways that do not include mental health advice. Just

make sure that you're helping in a way that does not make them feel like they're incompetent.

7. Nonverbally assure your friend or family member that you are ready to catch them when they fall. After you've created that safe space for them, make sure that they know that you're able and willing to catch the broken pieces of them if or when they fall apart. This doesn't mean that you verbally tell them that you're ready to handle their sharp edges; it simply means that you show up in a manner that does the speaking for you. Be confident, kind, and humble, and this will come across through your mannerisms.

8. Allow your friend or family member to make their own choices, even if they're different than the choices you would've made. I've probably said it a million times, but each person's journey through trauma is different, and they'll make different decisions than you would if you were in that situation. Remember, your role is not to judge or to force them to do something. Your role is to support them in the decisions they make, decisions that they're perfectly capable of making.

Though these eight steps exist, holding space for someone, especially when you've never done it before, might feel like you're floundering without any direction. Allow yourself to take a breath and remember that your only job is to let them know that they're accepted, that they belong, and that they're not alone. You're not responsible for fixing them. You're not responsible for the decisions they make. You're simply there to love them.

I want to finish this chapter by saying that holding space for someone who's very close to you is not easy. Their work in healing is hard, yes, but your work can be hard, too. It can be absolutely gut-wrenching to watch someone you love struggle. When I was going through my traumatic relationship with the individual I talked about at the beginning of the book, I got wrapped up in his pain and I did not take care of myself. I didn't know how to hold the space for him properly; instead, I decided to become the bearer of every one of his issues and place the responsibility of his life in my hands. If I would have known these eight tips, especially the fourth one, I firmly believe that he and I would have both come out of that relationship less scarred and less hurt. Beyond just knowing how to hold the space for someone else, make sure that someone is holding the space for you, too. It will be hard. You will need support, and your emotions will be running higher than normal because of the fact that you love the survivor. Make sure you have someone supporting you, too, and that will make holding the space for your friend or family member much easier and much more successful.

Chapter 19:
Resources for Finding Practitioners

☙❧

T hroughout the various chapters, I listed some links where you could find registered practitioners and such in the various therapeutic methods. For ease of reference, I've put them all in a list here:

- Support Groups: www.psychologyto-day.com/us/groups/trauma-and-ptsd
- EMDR: www.emdria.org/find-a-therapist/
- Craniosacral Therapy: www.iahp.com/pages/search/index.php
- Transcendental Meditation: www.tm.org (button in the upper righthand corner)
- Dance-Movement Therapy: www.adta.org/find-a-dmt
- Trauma-Sensitive Yoga:

www.traumasensitiveyoga.com/find-a-facilitator.html
- EAGALA Equine-Assisted Therapy: www.eagala.org/programs
- Epona Equine-Assisted Therapy: eponaquest.com/recommended-instructors/
- Therapy Dog Organizations: www.akc.org/sports/title-recognition-program/therapy-dog-program/therapy-dog-organizations
- Flower Essence Therapy Rescue Remedies: www.directlyfromnature.com/?Click=69584

Thank you for making it to the end of How To Heal*!*

〇〇

I really appreciate all of your feedback, and I love hearing what you have to say. I need your input to make the next version of this book and my future books better.

Please leave me a helpful review on Amazon letting me know what you thought of the book at: jessibeyerinternational.com/amazon

If you'd like to share your thoughts or story but aren't comfortable doing it on a public platform, feel free to send me a personal email at jessi@jessibeyerinternational.com or a direct message on Instagram @jessibeyerinternational.

- Jessi Beyer

Acknowledgements

ೞೋ

Whew! This book has been a labor of love, lots of time, and bunches of interviews. There are so many people that I can thank, and I'll do my best to give them all the recognition they deserve.

First of all, thank you to Josiah Biernat for your editing help! I know you're not the most avid self-help reader, but having someone come in, find the holes, and ask the questions I didn't answer made this book a whole lot better!

Secondly, thank you to Josiah (again) and Brian Armstrong for your extensive help with cover selection. I know I asked you pretty much every day which design you liked the best, but I really do appreciate your input!

Thirdly, thank you to every professional who I interviewed for this book: Amy, CJ, Tracey, Barbara, Molly, Kate, Gerry, Loey, Hilary, Lynn, Heather, and Sally. Your expertise is invaluable, and the helping hand you lend to so many people is nothing short of inspirational. Keep up the incredible work – you're truly saving lives.

Fourthly, thank you to every survivor I surveyed and

interviewed about your experience healing from trauma. You are so much stronger than you know, both for overcoming your personal demons and for contributing to a public work that aims to help others. I am so proud of each and every one of you!

Fifthly, thank you to my AMAZING book launch team! I'll be honest, I had absolutely no idea how to run a book launch team, but y'all were incredibly supportive and helped me so much during the month leading up to my launch. We couldn't have done this without you!

Last but certainly not least, thank YOU, my readers. I'll be honest, this book was written as much for my past self as it was for you, but knowing that you might find comfort, solace, and a path to healing from this warms my heart more than you could possibly know.

References

ตะฌๅ

Abraham, A., Sommerhalder, K., & Abel, T. (2009). Landscape and well-being: a scoping study on the health-promoting impact of outdoor environments. *International Journal Of Public Health*, *55*(1), 59-69. doi:10.1007/s00038-009-0069-z

Adverse Childhood Experiences (ACEs). Retrieved from https://www.cdc.gov/violenceprevention/childabuseandneglect/acestudy/index.html

American Psychiatric Association. (2013). *Posttraumatic Stress Disorder* [PDF] (p. 2).

Arnadottir, T., & Sigurdardottir, A. (2013). Is craniosacral therapy effective for migraine? Tested with HIT-6 Questionnaire. *Complementary Therapies In Clinical Practice*, *19*(1), 11-14. doi:10.1016/j.ctcp.2012.09.003

Barnes, V., Rigg, J., & Williams, J. (2013). Clinical Case Series: Treatment of PTSD With Transcendental Meditation in Active Duty Military Personnel. *Military Medicine*, *178*(7), e836-e840. doi: 10.7205/milmed-d-

12-00426

Benefits of the Human-Animal Bond. Retrieved from https://petpartners.org/learn/benefits-human-animal-bond/

Beyer, K., Kaltenbach, A., Szabo, A., Bogar, S., Nieto, F., & Malecki, K. (2014). Exposure to Neighborhood Green Space and Mental Health: Evidence from the Survey of the Health of Wisconsin. *International Journal Of Environmental Research And Public Health, 11*(3), 3453-3472. doi:10.3390/ijerph110303453

Blaschke, S., O'Callaghan, C., & Schofield, P. (2018). Nature-based supportive care opportunities: a conceptual framework. *BMJ Supportive & Palliative Care,* 5. doi:10.1136/bmjspcare-2017-001465

Brough, N., Lindenmeyer, A., Thistlethwaite, J., Lewith, G., & Stewart-Brown, S. (2015). Perspectives on the effects and mechanisms of craniosacral therapy: A qualitative study of users' views. *European Journal Of Integrative Medicine, 7*(2), 172-183. doi:10.1016/j.eujim.2014.10.003

Brunton, G. (2019). [Phone]. Minneapolis, Minnesota.

Campanini, M. (1997). Bach Flower Therapy: Results of a Monitored Study of 115 Patients. *La Medicina Biologica, 15*(2), 1-13.

Cristobal, K. (2018). Power of Touch: Working with Survivors of Sexual Abuse Within Dance/Movement Therapy. *American Journal Of Dance Therapy, 40*(1), 68-86. doi:10.1007/s10465-018-9275-7

Colebeck, L. (2019). [Phone]. Minneapolis, Minnesota.

Cram, J. A Convergence of Evidence: Flower Essence Therapy in the Treatment of Major Depression. *Calix, 1,* 89-106.

CST FAQs. Retrieved from https://www.upledger.com/therapies/faq.php

Davis, L., Hanson, B., & Gilliam, S. (2016). Pilot study of the effects of mixed light touch manual therapies on active duty soldiers with chronic post-traumatic stress disorder and injury to the head. *Journal Of Bodywork And Movement Therapies, 20*(1), 42-51. doi:10.1016/j.jbmt.2015.03.006

Del Castillo, A. *Upledger Institute Case Study CranioSacral Therapy - PTSD* [PDF] (p. 1). Upledger Institute. Retrieved from https://www.iahe.com/docs/articles/upledger-institute-case-study---craniosacral-ptsd.pdf

DePrekel, M. (2019). [Phone]. Minneapolis, Minnesota.

Devereaux, C. (2008). Untying the Knots: Dance/Movement Therapy with a Family Exposed to Domestic Violence. *American Journal Of Dance Therapy, 30*(2), 58-70. doi:10.1007/s10465-008-9055-x

Earles, J., Vernon, L., & Yetz, J. (2015). Equine-Assisted Therapy for Anxiety and Posttraumatic Stress Symptoms. *Journal Of Traumatic Stress, 28*(2), 149-152. doi:10.1002/jts.21990

Ernst, E. (2012). Craniosacral therapy: a systematic review of the clinical evidence. *Focus on Alternative and Complementary Therapies, 17*(4), 197-201. doi:10.1111/j.2042-7166.2012.01174.x

FAQ. Retrieved from https://eponaquest.com/about/faq/

Frumkin, H., Bratman, G., Breslow, S., Cochran, B., Kahn Jr, P., & Lawler, J. et al. (2017). Nature Contact and Human Health: A Research Agenda. *Environmental Health Perspectives*, *125*(7), 075001. doi:10.1289/ehp1663

Gray, A. (2001). The Body Remembers: Dance/Movement Therapy with an Adult Survivor of Torture. *American Journal Of Dance Therapy*, *23*(1), 29-43. doi:10.1023/A:1010780306585

Greenberg, P., Fournier, A., Sisitsky, T., Pike, C., & Kessler, R. (2015). The Economic Burden of Adults With Major Depressive Disorder in the United States (2005 and 2010). *The Journal Of Clinical Psychiatry*, *76*(02), 155-162. doi:10.4088/jcp.14m09298

Halberstein, R., DeSantis, L., Sirkin, A., Padron-Fajardo, V., & Ojeda-Vaz, M. (2007). Healing With Bach® Flower Essences: Testing a Complementary Therapy. *Complementary Health Practice Review*, *12*(1), 3-14. doi:10.1177/1533210107300705

Hall, W., & Doran, C. (2016). How Much Can the USA Reduce Health Care Costs by Reducing Smoking?. *PLOS Medicine*, *13*(5), e1002021. doi:10.1371/journal.pmed.1002021

Health and Economic Costs of Chronic Disease. (2019). Retrieved from https://www.cdc.gov/chronicdisease/about/costs/index.htm

Holthuis, K. (2018). "I do not feel like trash anymore.". *Flower Essence Society'S International E-*

Journal, 8-17.

How Much Does Therapy Cost?. (2014). [Blog]. Retrieved from https://www.goodtherapy.org/blog/faq/how-much-does-therapy-cost

Jäkel, A., & von Hauenschild, P. (2012). A systematic review to evaluate the clinical benefits of craniosacral therapy. *Complementary Therapies In Medicine*, *20*(6), 456-465. doi:10.1016/j.ctim.2012.07.009

Kearney, D., Malte, C., McManus, C., Martinez, M., Felleman, B., & Simpson, T. (2013). Loving-Kindness Meditation for Posttraumatic Stress Disorder: A Pilot Study. *Journal Of Traumatic Stress*, *26*(4), 426-434. doi:10.1002/jts.21832

Kratz, S., Kerr, J., & Porter, L. (2017). The use of CranioSacral therapy for Autism Spectrum Disorders: Benefits from the viewpoints of parents, clients, and therapists. *Journal Of Bodywork And Movement Therapies*, *21*(1), 19-29. doi:10.1016/j.jbmt.2016.06.006

Lee, M., Zaharlick, A., & Akers, D. (2011). Meditation and Treatment of Female Trauma Survivors of Interpersonal Abuses: Utilizing Clients' Strengths. *Families In Society: The Journal Of Contemporary Social Services*, *92*(1), 41-49. doi:10.1606/1044-3894.4053

Levine, B., & Land, H. (2015). A Meta-Synthesis of Qualitative Findings About Dance/Movement Therapy for Individuals With Trauma. *Qualitative Health Research*, *26*(3), 330-344. doi:10.1177/1049732315589920

Mackinnon, K. (2014). *Dana's Experience of Craniosacral*

Therapy [Video]. Retrieved from
https://www.youtube.com/watch?v=ZZ8yxO3WcEA

Mackinnon, K. (2019). [Video]. Minneapolis, Minnesota.

Moore, L., Mixon, S., & Jeffrey, H. (2019). [In person]. Forest Lake, Minnesota.

Morris, N. (2003). *Health, Well-Being and Open Space Literature Review* [PDF] (pp. 10-12). Edinburgh: Edinburgh College of Art and Heriot-Watt University.

Mueller, H. (2019). [In person]. St. Paul, Minnesota.

Nidich, S., O'Connor, T., Rutledge, T., Duncan, J., Compton, B., Seng, A., & Nidich, R. (2016). Reduced Trauma Symptoms and Perceived Stress in Male Prison Inmates through the Transcendental Meditation Program: A Randomized Controlled Trial. *The Permanente Journal*, *20*(4), 43-47. doi:10.7812/tpp/16-007

Nidich, S., Seng, A., Compton, B., O'Connor, T., Salerno, J., & Nidich, R. (2017). Transcendental Meditation and Reduced Trauma Symptoms in Female Inmates: A Randomized Controlled Study. *The Permanente Journal*, *21*(16), 39-43. doi:10.7812/tpp/16-008

Nordstrom-Loeb, B. (2019). [In person]. Minneapolis, Minnesota.

Perry, C., Perry, K., Boltuch, R., & Sisco, M. (2016). *Upledger CranioSacral Immersion Report for Dr. John E. Upledger Program for Military Post-Traumatic Stress* [PDF]. Retrieved from https://www.upledger.com/docs/2016-CranioSacral-Immersion-Program-Results.pdf

Plett, H. (2015). What it means to "hold space" for people,

plus eight tips on how to do it well [Blog]. Retrieved from https://heatherplett.com/2015/03/hold-space/

Polacek, C. (2019). [Email].

PTSD and CranioSacral Therapy. Retrieved from https://www.upledger.com/ptsd/

Rees, B., Travis, F., Shapiro, D., & Chant, R. (2014). Significant Reductions in Posttraumatic Stress Symptoms in Congolese Refugees Within 10 days of Transcendental Meditation Practice. *Journal Of Traumatic Stress*, *27*(1), 112-115. doi:10.1002/jts.21883

Rosenthal, J., Grosswald, S., Ross, R., & Rosenthal, N. (2011). Effects of Transcendental Meditation in Veterans of Operation Enduring Freedom and Operation Iraqi Freedom With Posttraumatic Stress Disorder: A Pilot Study. *Military Medicine*, *176*(6), 626-630. doi:10.7205/milmed-d-10-00254

Ross, D. (2010). Children with Learning Challenges: transforming core emotional trauma. *FES International Research Journal Online*, 25-28.

Salzberg, C. (2017). 4 Breathing-Based Meditation Techniques For A Stress-Less Life! [Blog]. Retrieved from https://basmati.com/2017/06/05/4-breathing-based-meditation-techniques-stress-less-life

Seppälä, E., Nitschke, J., Tudorascu, D., Hayes, A., Goldstein, M., & Nguyen, D. et al. (2014). Breathing-Based Meditation Decreases Posttraumatic Stress Disorder Symptoms in U.S. Military Veterans: A Randomized Controlled Longitudinal Study. *Journal Of Traumatic Stress*, *27*(4), 397-405.

doi:10.1002/jts.21936

Strunk, J. *A Brief Introduction to EMDR* [PDF] (pp. 1-3).

Sugeno, A. (2019). [Video]. Minneapolis, Minnesota.

Transcendental Meditation® Technique – Official Website. (2019). Retrieved from https://www.tm.org/home

The Upledger Institute International. Retrieved from https://www.upledger.com/index.php

Trauma- and Stressor-Related Disorders. (2013). *Diagnostic And Statistical Manual Of Mental Disorders.* doi:10.1176/appi.books.9780890425596.dsm07

Twohig-Bennett, C., & Jones, A. (2018). The health benefits of the great outdoors: A systematic review and meta-analysis of greenspace exposure and health outcomes. *Environmental Research, 166,* 628-637. doi:10.1016/j.envres.2018.06.030

Upledger, J., Kaplan, B., Bourne, R., & Zonderman, R. The effects of Upledger craniosacral therapy on post traumatic stress disorder symptomatology in Vietnam combat veterans. *Subtle Energies & Energy Medicine, 11*(2), 123-143.

U.S. Department of Justice. (2015). *Frequently Asked Questions about Service Animals and the ADA* [PDF]. Retrieved from https://www.ada.gov/regs2010/service_animal_qa.pdf

Vujanovic, A., Niles, B., Pietrefesa, A., Schmertz, S., & Potter, C. (2011). Mindfulness in the treatment of post-traumatic stress disorder among military veterans. *Professional Psychology: Research And Practice, 42*(1), 24-31. doi:10.1037/a0022272

Waelde, L., Thompson, J., Robinson, A., & Iwanicki, S. (2016). Trauma Therapists' Clinical Applications, Training, and Personal Practice of Mindfulness and Meditation. *Mindfulness*, *7*(3), 622-629. doi:10.1007/s12671-016-0497-9

Wetzler, G., Roland, M., Fryer-Dietz, S., & Dettmann-Ahern, D. (2017). CranioSacral Therapy and Visceral Manipulation: A New Treatment Intervention for Concussion Recovery. *Medical Acupuncture*, *29*(4), 239-248. doi:10.1089/acu.2017.1222

Wiedenhofer, S., Hofinger, S., Wagner, K., & Koch, S. (2016). Active Factors in Dance/Movement Therapy: Health Effects of Non-Goal-Orientation in Movement. *American Journal Of Dance Therapy*, *39*(1), 113-125. doi:10.1007/s10465-016-9240-2

Wilkins, T. (2019). [In person]. St. Paul, Minnesota.

Woolverton, M. (2019). [Phone]. St. Anthony, Minnesota.

Yang, W., Dall, T., Beronjia, K., Lin, J., Semilla, A., Chakrabarti, R., & Hogan, P. (2018). Economic Costs of Diabetes in the U.S. in 2017. *Diabetes Care*, *41*(5), 917-928. doi: 10.2337/dci18-0007